The Essential Guide to Game Audio

The Essential Guide to Game Audio

The Theory and Practice of
Sound for Games

**Steve Horowitz and
Scott Looney**

Focal Press
Taylor & Francis Group

NEW YORK AND LONDON

First published 2014
by Focal Press
70 Blanchard Road, Suite 402, Burlington, MA 01803

and by Focal Press
2 Park Square, Milton Park, Abingdon, Oxon OX14 4RN

Focal Press is an imprint of the Taylor & Francis Group, an informa business

Notices
Knowledge and best practice in this field are constantly changing. As new research and
experience broaden our understanding, changes in research methods, professional practices,
or medical treatment may become necessary.

Practitioners and researchers must always rely on their own experience and knowledge in
evaluating and using any information, methods, compounds, or experiments described herein.
In using such information or methods they should be mindful of their own safety and the
safety of others, including parties for whom they have a professional responsibility.

Product or corporate names may be trademarks or registered trademarks, and are used only for
identification and explanation without intent to infringe.

Library of Congress Cataloging-in-Publication Data
Horowitz, Steve, 1964–
The essential guide to game audio : the theory and practice of sound for games / Steve
  Horowitz and Scott R. Looney.
      pages cm
  1. Computer games—Programming.   2. Computer sound processing.   I. Title.
QA76.76.C672H678   2014
006.4'5—dc23   2013041385

ISBN: 978-0-415-70670-4 (pbk)
ISBN: 978-1-315-88679-4 (ebk)

Typeset in Myriad Pro
by Apex CoVantage, LLC

Printed in the USA

SUSTAINABLE
FORESTRY
INITIATIVE
Certified Chain of Custody
Promoting Sustainable Forestry
www.sfiprogram.org
SFI-01268

SFI label applies to the text stock

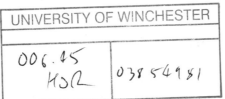

Contents

Acknowledgments

As the old saying goes, "sometimes it takes a village . . . ", so bearing that in mind we'd like to profusely thank the following folk:

Sean Connelly and Caitlin Murphy, and the whole team at Focal Press,
Kenneth Johnson and the whole crew at Zephyr Games,
Matt Donner and Greg Gordon, and the whole team at Pyramind,
Jeremy Engel for additional photography and graphic design,
Max Savage for application video editing,
and Adam Levenson from Levenson Arts.

We'd also like to thank all the awesome game audio pros for their contribution and fantastic viewpoints.

Special thanks to Bradley Hughes for getting the ball rolling.

And lastly, our families for love and support.

Foreword

A Word from Steve Horowitz

When I first got started making audio for games back in the early 1990s, I never expected to have such a diverse and varied career. I had no idea how much I would enjoy making crazy music and sounds for games or how much I would thrive on being a technical evangelist, deepening my knowledge of game theory, design and its impact on sound. Now, more than 20 years later, I see that the more things change, the more they stay the same. When someone asked for "audio" back in the day, they meant all the music, sound design and voice-over in a title—everything, basically. As the years progressed, composers, sound designers and recording engineers have all developed increased specialization. This is especially true for big budget console titles, where there's so much media that it's no longer reasonable for one person to do it all. Enter the new millennium—a new influx of mobile, social and online gaming has changed the landscape once again, and these titles require a more complete knowledge of more than one discipline. It is my hope that this book will become a valuable tool in the development of well-rounded audio designers, ready to meet any real-world challenge.

Whether I was working as a freelance composer or as the audio director for Nickelodeon Digital, over the years I have been truly blessed to work with many "off the charts" talents, from top notch producers and programmers, to voice-over actors and fellow audio geeks. They are, simply stated, some of the best, brightest and funniest folks walking around on the planet. I've learned a lot from them and I am a far richer person as a result. One such human is my co-author Scott Looney. It is hard to put into words how fruitful my collaborations with Mr. Looney have been. Aside from being a fantastic piano player and composer in his own right, his dedication to audio implementation, and fearlessness in diving into uncharted waters has made this book and the application that accompanies it, far richer than I could ever have imagined. Scott has more than 10 years of experience teaching and developing curriculum and his insight and input have been invaluable. Our relative strengths and weaknesses balance each other out in a very enriching and productive way, and working with him on this and many other projects has been a pure joy!

So, please take advantage of our 20 plus years of experience, along with our classroom tested teaching method. Our hope is that you will use it to create a firm foundation, and acquire the skills needed to succeed in the wacky world of sound for games!

A Note from Scott Looney

I've been involved with teaching digital audio-based concepts for over 13 years, and interactive audio for beginners for over eight of those years. I have always strived to explain complex concepts in simple ways, and this book is a logical extension of those efforts. A lot of the books I've read on the subject of game audio treat it as something massively technical—something akin to electronic alchemy—where only the anointed few are allowed to understand the mysteries at the heart of the subject. Others get involved in the minutiae of what sample libraries or microphones or audio setups someone has. While that bears some importance as to how you'll work, they are essentially putting the cart before the horse. To my mind, the most important thing is to first grasp the basic concepts of game audio and what it means when you work in a non-linear world. This fact needs to be absorbed and ingested before you can go on to talk about any of the specifics afterwards.

In this book and accompanying App, I think we've simplified the concepts involved without dumbing them down, and provided numerous contextualized examples (written, visual and interactive). If you come from a linear production background, I believe this book will get you up to speed on game audio in a reasonable amount of time. Together we've done our best to make the experience of the book and the App both informative and fun. We've certainly had a lot of fun writing it for sure, and I think the results will speak for themselves, as we begin a new chapter of game audio education.

My co-author Steve Horowitz has been working in the game audio trenches so long that they were barely gullies when he started. He's seen a lot of dynamic changes in the industry over the years, and for him the experience isn't a brand new one—these issues have a cyclical nature to them. I have enjoyed working with him immensely, serving in a wide variety of roles, and the combination of our efforts is far, far greater than it would be if we each took our own separate path. I feel incredibly blessed to have been given this opportunity, and here's to future collaboration!

How to Use This Book and The Application

The TCI Method Explained

This book is meant to be used in connection with the *Essential Guide to Game Audio* application. We have developed both the book and application to be functional in their own right. However, the content is most effective and useful when the written materials, videos and interactive examples are joined together.

It is highly recommended that you download the application first!

The application is available for free via the iTunes Store. If you have no iOS device, we have also made some content available to you via our Focal Press website page at www.focalpress.com/cw/Horowitz.

As you work your way through the levels (chapters) of this book, follow along inside the application. The icons described below will let you know exactly when there is content available to view or interact with.

THEORY

All knowledge starts with a conceptual theory of some kind. We take the most basic concepts at the heart of game audio and we find ways to show the concepts a number of times and in a variety of ways—via text, via image and by video tutorials. Material in green boxes delineates the important **written concepts** in the text for each level of the book.

This icon indicates when there is useful video content that supplements the text.

COMPREHENSION

The logical application of theory is benefitted by different assessment methods that aid the learning process. We have provided short interactive Quizzes for every level inside the App, as well as a number of Word Search examples that reinforce the terminology and concepts being taught.

This icon, if present, will guide you to the Word Search example for the level.

INTERACTION

In order to learn about what is essentially a non-linear and experiential medium, you really need to encounter the concept firsthand within the gaming environment. It does you no favors to play examples of game music or sound, and just imagine what it will be like in the game. Instead we immerse you in a game-like setting that illustrates the concepts in a more engaging and fun way!

This icon will guide you to the Interactive Quiz available in the App. These are available at the end of every Level/Chapter in the book.

This icon will alert you to go to the application and explore complete, **real time interactive environments** that highlight book concepts.

Note For Educators

This book represents the knowledge base of the first generation of game audio practitioners. These are the folks who have been in the trenches for many many years, and are just now starting to put together the roadmap and develop solid education models for game sound, based on their extensive years of experience. This practical understanding of the unique workflow of sound in games and what makes it different from film and TV, is crucial to students. It should also prove invaluable to the teacher tasked with creating a curriculum in sound for games at their institution. We have attempted to structure the book and application as a complete resource guide for educators. Each chapter (referred to as a Level, in homage to games) comes with clear learning objectives and outcomes.

In this book, we have tried very hard to break down basic concepts and only include what we consider to be the most essential knowledge in the field. We hope to strip out the noise and get to the important points as quickly and clearly as possible. Over the years of teaching the subject in the classroom we have developed what we believe to be the most effective educational method for the subject. This involves solidifying the concepts presented in the book with an interactive hands-on experience. We've developed and included an interactive iOS application and examples that go hand-in-hand with the written text to greater enhance the student's understanding. What better way to learn about sound for games, than inside a game?

You may be in a classroom situation where not all students have access to iOS devices. To accommodate this situation we have set up a website: www. focalpress.com/cw/Horowitz. Unfortunately not all the App's content is available online currently, but we have provided the essential interactive examples that will allow you to teach to the method effectively. We also understand that students have different learning styles and we have done our best to accommodate these differences in our overall methodology by keeping the framework focused and flexible. Your feedback in this regard is desired and valuable to us, so we have set up an area on the website where you can leave comments, ideas, thoughts and concerns.

Introduction
Why You Need This Book

Unless you've been living in a concrete bunker in an undisclosed location for the last 20 years or so, you probably know why you are reading this book. Games are a huge mega business these days, and the industry has been steadily growing over the years. There have been a few major downturns in this roller coaster ride we call gaming, and if you happen to own the original *E.T. the Extra-Terrestrial* game for the Atari 2600 (you know—the one that single-handedly caused the bottom to fall out of the video game industry in 1982?) then you know what I'm talking about.

The games business as a whole is a dynamic, thriving and turbulent industry to work in. This has been true since its inception. Since so much of the industry is based on cutting-edge technology, youth and speculation, it is no surprise that change comes violently and rapidly. To the practitioners of a career in games and interactive media, this change can be maddening, but it is in many ways essential to an art form that is still defining its role in popular culture.

As a society we are making the transition to a more virtual world. People just don't seem interested in tangible technology anymore (remember CDs? Cassettes?). Physical distribution is going away and there is even a new word being bandied about—Gamification! From healthcare to global climate change, we are seeing the forms and ideas of gameplay invade our everyday world. From 'power ups' to coupons, games seem to be with us to stay.

The cartridge for the ill-fated *E.T. the Extra-Terrestrial* game from Atari, widely believed to be one of the contributing factors to the video game industry crash in the early 1980s.

Maybe you're a complete newcomer to sound for games, or perhaps you are already working creating audio for traditional linear media like film and television—or it could be you are involved with record production and want to get a clear picture of how to apply your skills to the game market. For all of these cases and more, we say "Good news weary traveler, you have come to the right place!"

Original music, creative sound design and brilliant voice-over is essential to making good games. That's where you come in. Professionals at all levels are needed to create solid audio experiences, and accordingly, must be given a solid foundation. Much of the skill set from film, TV and other forms of linear media can be applied to making sound for games. However, a complete understanding of what makes games and interactive media unique is essential to developing your art and craft, and building your career.

Opportunity Knocks!

The good news is that in 2007, the game industry overtook film in total gross receipts, and so far, has not looked back. More people around the globe are playing games than ever before and the

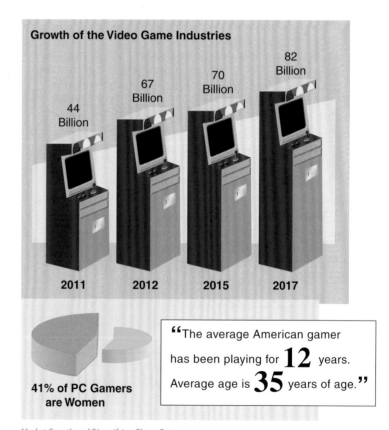

Market Growth and Diversifying Player Base.

demographics of these players are changing and just might surprise you. Not just a pastime for young men with giant thumbs anymore, games are invading every part of our society. Older people (such as I), women, and an enormous variety of humans are getting into the game.

The worldwide video game industry is set to grow upwards to $82 billion by 2017, thanks to the combined growth of portable, PC, and online video games, according to market researcher DFC Intelligence. It estimates that games were a $67 billion business in 2012.

According to the Entertainment Software Rating Board (ESRB) almost 41 percent of PC gamers are women. When comparing today's industry climate with that of 20 years ago, women and many adults in general are more inclined to be using products in the industry. While the market for teen and young adult men is still a strong market, it is the other demographics that are posting significant growth. Apparently, the average American gamer has been playing for 12 years, and is now, on average, 35 years of age.

These numbers suggest that the boom in the video game industry is not restricted to the United States. In fact, if we look at worldwide numbers, we see that the video gaming market (not including hardware) is projected to grow by more than 100 percent. It turns out that every other region of the world is expected to experience more growth than the US over the next five years, which probably represents the relative maturity of the US market more than any American lack of time, resources, or interest in decapitating aliens.

Innovation has been taking artistic forms as well. Games are now competing on a level footing with film and TV and other forms of visual media. Various organizations have been trying to influence the film and TV and music industries to recognize achievements in video games, and specifically audio and music for these games. This has begun to bear some fruit lately.

In 2012 the composer for the video game *Journey* (published by Sony Interactive), Austin Wintory, was nominated for a Grammy by the NARAS (National Academy of the Recording Arts and Sciences) in the category of Best Score Soundtrack for Visual Media. This was not game music's first brush with Grammy recognition, however. Composer Christopher Tin actually won a Grammy for Best Instrumental Arrangement Accompanying Vocalist(s) in 2011 for his song 'Baba Yetu' featured in the game *Civilization IV*. This was the first time a song from a video game has ever won a Grammy.

Composer Austin Wintory received a Grammy nomination in 2012 for Best Score Soundtrack for Visual Media for his evocative music for the game *Journey* (2012 by thatgamecompany, produced by Sony Santa Monica and published by Sony Computer Entertainment America).

Credit: Jeremy Keith (adactio).

Groups like The Game Audio Network Guild (GANG) also try to create industry recognition through annual awards for quality music and audio design for both established and new composers and sound designers. Live performances of game music scores by well-known orchestras and groups like Video Games Live spread awareness of game music as a viable concert phenomenon. The experience for fans of classic games is electrifying—a full orchestra onstage starts playing the theme of a well-known game like *Zelda* for instance, and suddenly hundreds of fans are cheering and yelling for their favorite themes.

In the last few years, online gaming has skyrocketed. Thanks to gaming consoles, smartphones, and social networking sites like Facebook, in combination with increasingly high speed internet connectivity. All the major game consoles and even the PC have moved heavily over to online gaming due to various services offering seamless license management of online purchases.

The Portable Market Is Exploding

Remember the iPad? Well thanks to its emergence, combined with increasingly sophisticated smartphones like the iPhone, video games now have a new, powerful, portable platform well suited for less standard gaming markets in addition to the expected demographics.

Though the portable gaming industry has long existed, and gaming on phones and personal digital assistants (PDAs) has been possible for at least 20 years, these new devices offer considerably better graphics capabilities than their predecessors, and they also offer revolutionary multi-touch interfaces. The result has been a huge increase in the number of small, independent companies that develop games for iOS and distribute them online digitally via the iTunes store.

With all this talk though, we mustn't forget Android, the most popular mobile device operating system (and one developed using open source technology). Although devices using Android are lagging behind devices on iOS in sales of games at the moment, their potential user bases are larger.

There are not many things in life you can be sure of, but the growth and transformation of gaming might just be a smart bet. With motion sensor, eye and neuro controllers starting to hit the market, we can already see a bright future in advanced gaming systems that are still in their infancy. New games, new genres, and new styles are coming, not to mention new software and hardware specifications. The future looks bright, and without a doubt, it will need sound—and sound professionals. That's your cue to turn the page, because the future is now!

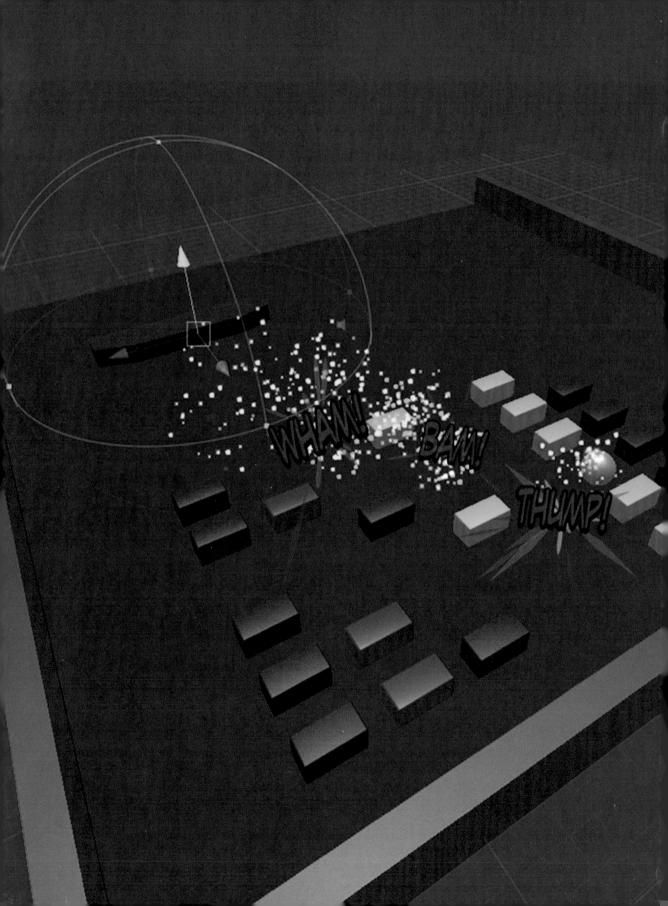

AAA (Animation, Art, Audio)
Making Sense of Sound for Games

What's a Platform? •
A Video Game's Structure •
Is it a Story or is it Interactivity? •
"Make It So"—The Game Controller •
Let's Make Some Noise •

Learning Outcomes:
Understand what makes audio for games unique •
Develop a basic overview of hardware and software for games •
Gain insight into emergent behavior •

What's a Platform?

The physical electronic systems used to play video games are known as **platforms**. The term describes the electronic or computer hardware that runs the software that allows a video game to operate. A platform may be anything from a large mainframe computer to a small handheld device. The platform may also be called a **system**.

Video games are played on several different types of platforms:

A variety of platforms on which games can run.

7

A VIDEO GAME'S STRUCTURE

As audio people, It is important to understand why games are the way they are. We need to keep the picture in mind as to what exactly is going on under the hood in a video game. So let's break it down into some basic observations.

Video games are by nature interactive. This means that when you provide some kind of input into the game, you get a response of some kind.

A really basic non-game analogy is simply typing something on a device. When you press physical keys on your device's keyboard (or on the glass of your tablet or smartphone), the character corresponding to the character you typed appears immediately on the screen.

A slightly more complex analogy of interactivity would be visiting a link to a website. When the user clicks a link on a web page, the action sends a command to a server to load the web page or the object associated with that link.

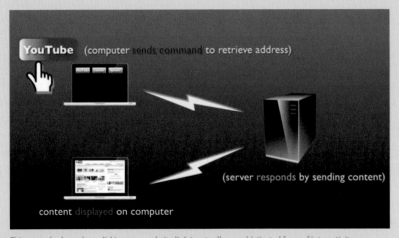

This example shows how clicking on a website link is actually a sophisticated form of interactivity.

A video game works in a similar manner; it uses the interaction between the player and an electronic or computerized device to generate feedback that is displayed on the video screen. Initially, games consisted of simple interactions, but as these interactions have gained complexity, they have produced increasingly rich entertainment experiences.

Credit: Tobii Technology.

Arcade

An arcade game is a self-contained electronic device that typically plays only one game, which is housed in a freestanding cabinet. The arcade games were the first commercially successful platform, and enjoyed huge popularity in the 1980s. Although their popularity has since greatly diminished, they are still being made today.

Console

A console game is played on an electronic device called a console. This device usually connects to a television set or other monitor for its video output. The console was the first major gaming platform that emerged separately from the arcade. You may also hear the term **next-gen console**, which refers to newer video game platforms, that may or may not actually be consoles, but are called as such because the term itself evokes such a powerful connotation with dedicated gamers.

Credit: Digitpedia.

PC

A PC game is any game played on a personal computer. This platform has seen a lot of shifts over the years, the PC game market is still dominated by Windows, although the changeover to Intel processors by Apple has now made it possible to port games much more easily to Mac. In addition, Linux has emerged in recent years as a viable game platform. The Linux OS is similar in many ways to Apple's Mac OS X, and the online game vendor Valve (makers of *Team Fortress 2* and *Portal*, amongst others) has announced full support for it in its Steam online game distribution service. Will this lead to a three way tie between Windows, Mac and Linux? Probably not, but you never know . . .

Credit: David Brown.

Handheld

A handheld game is played on a self-contained, portable electronic device that is designed specifically to be held in a player's hands. Although there were other small, simple dedicated gaming handhelds created by toy makers like Mattel, it was the Nintendo GameBoy that was the first well-known device to establish a viable market for handheld devices. Since then, there have been many others, like the Play Station Portable and Nintendo DS, to name just a few.

Credit: Mirko Tobias Schaefer.

Mobile

A mobile game is played on any device that is portable and self contained, like a handheld, but unlike handhelds the device is not created primarily for gaming purposes. This platform had its beginnings in simple cell phone games like *Snake*, but has greatly expanded with the advent of smartphones and especially tablets using iOS, Android, and Windows Mobile. The mobile platform is expanding at a huge rate at the moment. Games for these devices may be categorized as PC games, but this is really a misnomer, since the operating systems for PC and mobile devices are different.

Credit: Josué Goge.

Multiplatform Games

Recently, gaming has started to move away from running on only one platform. Historically a Mac version of a Windows game (a fairly uncommon occurrence) would be the most common example of a multiplatform game. This is normally referred to as a port. Since Mac and PC platforms now share a lot of hardware similarities (using Intel processors for instance) it becomes easier and easier to create Mac and PC versions of top-selling games.

Web-Based Games

One of the very first examples of going multiplatform is using an engine that has the same visual interface on every machine. Tools like Adobe's Flash were used frequently to make interactive media and games, and because the finished work could run on Mac or PC identically, the experience for gamers was the same. The tradition of web-based gaming is currently evolving away from using Flash and is more and more dependent on HTML5 and Javascript. Its ambition to provide the same gaming experience on PCs is further expanded with the addition of mobile devices like smartphones and tablets.

Cloud Gaming

This logical extension of multiplatform gaming is a very recent phenomenon in gaming. Although some games are made for multiple platforms, cloud games are quite literally the exact same game, but made available for a large variety of devices via a single online service. Players of these games can play them on any device the cloud service supports, and the service keeps track of the player's progress so that they don't have to start over again when they switch to a new device—the service simply resizes the game screen and resources for the appropriate hardware platform.

Credit: Wim Vandenbussche and Romain Guy.

IS IT A STORY OR IS IT INTERACTIVITY?

Let's take a few moments to discuss the basic theories of video games. Even though computer scientists have studied video games from a technical position for a while now, the coverage and analysis of video games as an artistic medium is relatively new. There are two primary ways in which video games are analyzed these days.

Video Games as Stories

One group of people regard a game as something related to a book, a play or other media based on a story. Those interested in tying the concept of gaming as an extension to storytelling are called **narrativists.** They tend to regard video games as complex "cyberdramas" through which players can become other people and participate in other worlds. Of course, many games may have multiple conclusions and results due to the aspect of choice in the game. For narrativists this puts a video game into the category of interactive fiction.

Video Games as an Interactive Experience

The other group of people regard games primarily from the basis of the interactive structure within the game itself. Every game comes with its own set of rules and restrictions as to how the game should be played. These people are known as **ludologists**, and they look mainly at how the structure of the game places demands and restrictions on the player, and how the player then navigates their way through the restrictions in the game. These restrictions can then affect the social and artistic qualities of the game as a result.

Video Games are Emergent

In spite of the fact that each of these groups have differing viewpoints on the basis of what games are, they do tend to agree that most games depend on emergent principles. The term refers to complex outcomes that can result from the interaction of simple rules.

A rather beautiful example of this is the forming of snowflakes. Snowflakes form when water from clouds freezes, and the method in which they freeze, the temperature, the wind direction, each of these are simple factors that result in a staggering level of complexity and diversity. In fact it's so complex that no one snowflake looks like another.

There are two types of emergence commonly referred to by scholars, **intentional** and **unintentional**. Intentional emergence is something that has largely been designed or engineered. The results can be complex, but in effect everything has been calculated. You tend to know what's likely to happen given a set of basic rules. Unintentional emergence means that something arises unexpectedly from these simple rules, possibly even appearing to be random, or something close to it.

This snowflake is an example of emergent behavior in nature.
Credit: Andrew Magill.

Plants vs. Zombies offers a good example of a current game that displays intentional emergent behavior. The simple choices that a player makes early in the game lead to a complex set of circumstances and behaviors as the game progresses from level to level. The programmers and designers of this game have laid out a set of rules to create countless variations and even some unpredictable outcomes.

Plants vs Zombies from Popcap Games is a popular casual game that displays emergent behavior.

To describe the game briefly: the object of the game is to protect your house from wave after wave of invading zombies—don't you just hate it when that happens? On the right-hand side of the screen zombies come through your hedge and head for the house in single file—they are quite polite and organized. On the left-hand side is your house and above your house is a menu bar where you can select from different objects that help you to perform specific tasks, like planting sunflowers that spit out little balls that knock the zombies over, or collecting sunlight for energy. These simple events and interactions multiply as you move from level to level in the game. Zombies learn to jump over obstacles and other interesting things unfold so that by the time you get a few levels into it, complexity abounds.

Now, to bring us around to the topic of audio, this whole scenario presents an audio designer with a very interesting audio puzzle. Namely, how do we create a satisfying experience for the player when we don't know when or in what order things will happen in the game? Since objects can be combined by the player in any order, we also have no idea how all these possible combinations will unfold over time as the player moves through the game, and the music and sound effects must support this evolution. As you can see, this process is very different from linear media, like film or TV, and this is just one example of interactivity in games.

Okay, so what does unintentional emergence look like? A game glitch is a pretty good example of this type of emergent gameplay—objects in a game restricted to simple rules somehow produce unintended outcomes than what the designers had originally had in mind. Injecting the human player into the game also contributes tremendously to unintentionally emergent behavior. For example, players can take advantage of these glitches in order to improve their score in a game. Special controller button combinations in games like *Halo 2* would give you faster gun access after being in a melée, giving you an edge over other players. Emergent behavior can also result from using items in unexpected ways. An example of this is using the rocket launcher in *Quake* to vault the player up into the air, by firing it at the ground.

The cast of characters from *This Spartan Life:* a machinima talk show set in the game world of Halo.

Another extremely artistic result of unintentional emergence in gameplay is the phenomenon called **machinima**. Imagine your average multiplayer first-person shooter game. Basically you're a camera, moving around in the gamespace. Now, if you encounter another player in that space, you are, in effect, filming a 3D animated character as they are moving around and if you don't simply kill the player, you just become a cameraperson following them around. Games like *Quake* developed small clubs of players who would tape their progress and sometimes these led to little comedy bits. Eventually machinima developed out of this (the term was coined in 2002 by Hugh Hancock, the founder of Strange Company) and became a viable means of expression. There are by now dozens of examples of quality material made from this concept—from abstract films to talk shows filmed and produced in game space—all of which essentially derived randomly from, you could say, a misuse of the game, that caught on.

The reason we're going on a long time about this is because the study of emergent behavior is extremely important for understanding a game's structure. Emergence is a common concept taught in game design and artificial intelligence (AI) classes. One well recommended book on this subject is author Penny Sweetser's *Emergence in Games* (Charles River Media).

Let's leave behind how games are designed for now, and move into discussing how games work. How does the player interact with a game device?

"Make It So"—The Game Controller

To get interaction from a game platform, the player needs an input device of some kind. The input device for console games is referred to as a **game controller**. This controller varies across platforms. It might have only a button and a joystick, or it might have many buttons and multiple joysticks. In games on non-dedicated platforms (hardware that is not designed specifically for gaming), the controller might be a computer keyboard, a mouse, or, on more recent touch devices, an onscreen interface that the player manipulates with his or her finger.

Game controllers can come in a wide variety of shapes and sizes. Clockwise from top left: Xbox controller; Playstation controller; Nintendo Power Glove; Logitech Driving Force; Kinect for Xbox360; Wii Remote and Nunchuck. Center: The classic Atari 2600 joystick.
Credit: Jeremy Engel.

Now, although games use these types of devices, there are other methods besides controllers to interact with and provide information to players. Chief among these methods is the use of sound effects and music to provide emotional and informational context and cues within a game's various levels. Games almost universally use audio, which is provided by internal devices, such as sound cards or chips embedded in circuit boards, and external sound-reproduction devices, such as speakers and headphones.

Input devices are radically changing as well. Although innovative controllers have existed for video games, in the past they did not often achieve popularity enough to serve as a good reason for owning a game console.

This changed in 2006 with the release of the Nintendo Wii, a radical new controller featuring a sophisticated infrared camera, plus an array of motion detectors and accelerometers all housed in a special remote. At last, you could play virtual tennis or golf and use considerably more realistic actions while doing so, as well as have great lightsaber battles! As amazing, original and successful as this innovation was, it was followed less than 5 years later by an even larger concept (metaphorically and literally)—that of using the player themselves as a controller. This is what the Kinect from Microsoft does, by using a few cameras and other sensors to detect the positions of the player. The Kinect has been a real boon to physically active games like *Dance Dance Revolution* or sports like snow or skate boarding. Now you can jump over chasms, clamber up walls, open doors. The future has indeed arrived . . .

Companies are investing in the research and development of all types of input devices to facilitate user interaction with video game environments. Inventors are using sites like Kickstarter to create these. One such device is the Oculus Rift, a pair of goggles with two LCD screens that the player wears, immersing themselves in the game environment. This device can also do head tracking, so when the player turns their head the view in the game also changes. At the cutting edge of technology, some researchers are exploring the use of human eye movement (also called gaze tracking), and recently biofeedback of different kinds.

One such development is the advent of brain controlled interfaces such as the Emotive controller and the Neurosky. The Emotive is an interface that has numerous contacts that each monitor the level of electrical activity in that part of the brain, and these can be used to control aspects of a game or other interactive setup.

Composer Richard Warp has recently managed to develop a system to connect the Emotive headset to a Yamaha Disklavier, a modern, MIDI controlled version of a player piano, in order to generate acoustic music controlled directly by the brain. Look Ma, no hands!

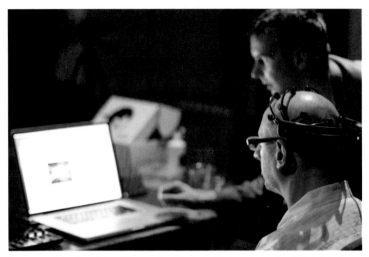

Composer and developer Richard Warp works with a test subject wearing an Emotiv Brain interface. These types of controllers, though still somewhat novel, are making inroads into traditional game platforms, and the market is expanding as interfaces like this become more affordable.
Credit: Nick Benavides.

Let's Make Some Noise

Regardless of the game type or platform, sound is a vital part of the gaming experience. This field usually falls into one of three broad categories: sound effects, voice-overs, and music. Most video games contain some amount of all three elements. Certain genres might have a lot of dialogue for example, others not so much. Most games will have at least one kind of sound effect, although the exceptions to that rule are the earliest games back in the later 1960s and early 1970s, which were completely silent. It wouldn't be worth dedicating a whole book to the craft of creating audio for silent games, but I think that probably goes without saying.

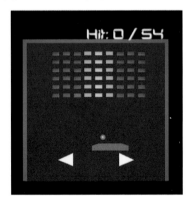

However, we can use silence to our advantage in our quest for understanding game audio. Imagine what the experience would be of playing a game without audio. Sound interesting?

Conclusion

Sound for games is not a single discipline, but a combination of disciplines that all come together to create a complete sound design. You may just be interested in one of these areas such as music, but a complete understanding of the overall system is essential to creating satisfying game audio experiences.

In this chapter we have also tried to give you a basic grounding in the state of the game industry as a whole. It is vital that you are aware of the basic business trends in games—all this information is part of being a good game audio citizen, and frankly a large part of what will get you hired in the field.

Unlike film, TV and other forms of linear media, each game you work on is uniquely individual, with rules and characteristics that define how the interaction, and thus the audio, functions in that world. Audio people have to look at issues of game design critically in order to create satisfying aural landscapes. I encourage you to think of yourself as a audio explorer. Who knows—you just might find that the technology of games is far more fascinating than you ever imagined!

Find out for yourself by going over to the App, and in the main classroom area, simply click on the Holo Deck and choose Breakout. Have fun!

The Interactive Quiz for this Level is available in the App. In the main Classroom, click on the Quiz book to test your knowledge!

On the Road— to NOW!

A Brief History of Games and Game Audio

Learning Outcomes:

Understand the evolution of key audio systems and essential developments ·

Distinguish between different platforms, genres, and technological stages ·

Comprehend technical limitations and how they shape audio development ·

Let's take a brief look at a few of the more notable achievements in gaming during this period.

The First Video Games

In 1948 Thomas T. Goldsmith, Jr., and Estle Ray Mann created one of the earliest known video games. Based on radar display technology, the cathode-ray tube used an analog device to simulate the experience of firing a missile at targets. Knobs and buttons allowed the player to control the missile, which was represented on screen by a vector-drawn dot.

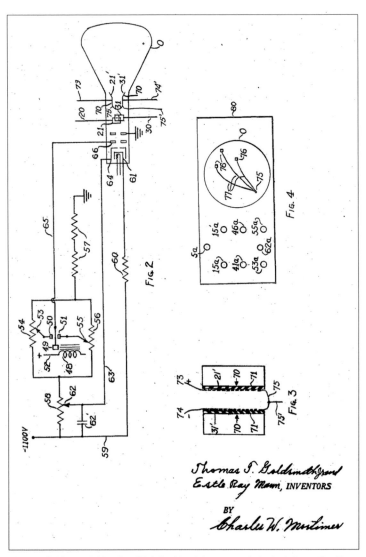

Schematic for Thomas Goldsmith and Estle Ray Mann's Amusement device in 1947, considered by most to be the earliest video game. Image courtesy of Thomas Goldsmith Estate.

MORE OR LESS

The history of sound in video games is the story of doing more with less—it's also the story of unforgettable themes and creative ingenuity. How can an orchestra fit in 36KB? How much music can fit on a CD-ROM? How can a PC game make any sounds at all? These are all real-world problems that needed to be solved at one time or another.

Just like the first movies, the first games were silent and had no sound at all. Gradually, however, creative hardware engineers figured out ways to make the earliest computer chips generate primitive sounds and effects in the 1970s. The sophistication of the hardware and software, as well as the methods involved in composing for this new medium, changed accordingly.

The development of game audio solutions follows a repeatable loop that keeps regenerating. Even today, we see the same thing. These days, consoles with DVD-quality sound and orchestral soundtracks sit on the shelf side-by-side with handheld devices that can only trigger small banks of sounds and compressed low bit rate audio. Composers and sound designers for this medium once again find themselves having to work within significant limitations.

Because of the rapidly changing formats that are used in creating games, as well as the pace of technological development, the development of sound for games has been and continues to be a lot like the Wild Wild West.

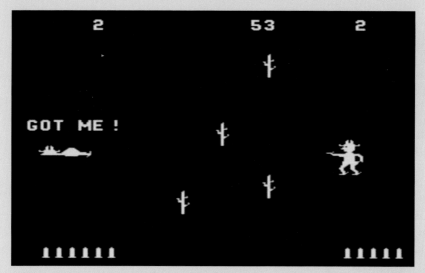

Screenshot from the arcade game *Gun Fight* (1976 Taito/Midway).

Nevertheless, we will bravely venture forth and try to make sense of the jungle of game audio history. You might be surprised to find out what's old, is new again!

1940–1970: THE SILENT ERA OF VIDEO GAMES

From the start, video games were made by computer programmers, the people who had the most access to the technology. Video-game development on university mainframe computers began in the late 1950s but blossomed in the early to mid-1970s. Because these games were not distributed commercially or regarded as serious endeavors, records remain of only the most popular of these games. The programmers who wrote these games—usually students—did so illicitly on expensive university-owned computers, so they were not eager to advertise the results. These explorations, however, became part of the DNA of the modern video-game industry.

A reproduction of *OXO* (noughts and crosses), originally designed in 1952.

OXO (1952)

In 1952, A.S. Douglas at the University of Cambridge developed *OXO*, a graphical version of tic-tac-toe (or noughts and crosses), to demonstrate his thesis on human–computer interaction. In *OXO*, the player competed directly against the EDSAC (Electronic Delay Storage Automatic Calculator), a computer that used a cathode-ray tube to create a visual display of memory contents.

Spacewar! (1961)

Spacewar! was a two-player game in which each player fired at the other from a spacecraft the player controlled. A star in the center of the screen created an obstacle for the crafts. Considered the first influential computer game, *Spacewar!* was eventually distributed with certain new mainframe computers and traded on the (then) primitive Internet.

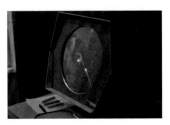

Spacewar! (1962) is one of the most well-known early mainframe-based computer games.
Credit: Joi Ito, Wikimedia.

Magnavox Odyssey (1972): The Earliest Home Video Console

In 1966, Ralph Baer, who had emerged as a video game pioneer in the 1950s, created the Magnavox Odyssey, the first home console game system, in 1972. Although it had no sound, the tennis game available with this system became the inspiration for the smash hit arcade game *Pong*.

Magnavox Odyssey, the first commercial game console, designed by Ralph Baer. The tennis game it featured was the main inspiration for Atari's *Pong*.

1970–1980: Early Arcade Games and Consoles

As we move into the 1970s we begin to hear the first primitive bleeps and bloops made by the first arcade games. At this point these sounds are created with hardware chips and the sounds are programmed using oscillators and basic tone generators like sine and square waves. Sound designers and composers of this era are very technically oriented, frequently being electrical engineers, and the act of creating these sounds involves a lot of complexity and is in many ways similar to programming computers.

Pong (1972): The First Arcade Video Game—With Sound!

The name Atari is often associated with the earliest arcade games. Founder Nolan Bushnell got his start making *Computer Space*, a version of *Spacewar!*, for a different company, but soon created Atari, convinced that video games were the future of entertainment.

Atari's first big success was *Pong*. Atari engineer Allan Alcorn originally programmed *Pong* as an exercise based on versions of a simple paddle tennis game Bushnell had seen on the Magnavox Odyssey game console. The first *Pong* prototype used an ordinary black-and-white TV installed in a four-foot-tall cabinet.

During development, Bushnell decided the game should provide sound effects and feedback, so Alcorn used a sync generator to create a primitive sound set. When Atari tested *Pong* at a local bar, Andy Capp's Tavern, the response was extremely favorable. The game itself was popular enough, but the digital sounds attracted crowds curious to discover the source of the noise.

Pong became one of the first arcade video games, the first to use sound, and the best-selling game to that point. In the process, it propelled Atari to preeminence in the brand new field of arcade video games.

An original *Pong* Console.
Credit: Rob Boudon.

So how does the sound work in the game? There are only three sounds in a *Pong* game: First is a short low pitched blip, that plays when the ball hits the side walls. Next is a longer and higher pitched blip when the ball strikes your paddle. And the last is a higher pitched bleep that gets triggered when you score a point. Simple, raw and quite elegant when you factor in how it was made.

Pong also became a home console game that spawned dozens of clones and led to the first video game slump. Atari led the industry out of this stagnant period with the first significant video game console with a sound chip, the Atari VCS or 2600.

The Atari VCS or 2600: this was the company's first and most well-known game console.

Atari 2600 (1977)

Unlike other self-contained home game consoles, which had limited functions, this version contained a complete central processing unit (CPU). This was combined with a chip for random-access memory (RAM), or short-term memory, and input/output (I/O). Atari also designed a display and sound chip called the TIA (Television Interface Adaptor), and added a fourth chip for CMOS (semiconductor) function. This four-chip design allowed Atari to make units inexpensively. The inclusion of RAM meant that players could change the game by loading different programs.

The sounds that the VCS (later known as the 2600) makes are quite quirky, raw and unlike anything anyone had ever heard come out of a TV. To give you an idea of the state of its audio capabilities, the 2600 featured 2 channels of 1-bit monaural sound along with a 4-bit volume control. You read right, 1 whole bit!! Nevertheless, to game aficionados the sound of the Atari 2600 is immediately recognizable, and especially sought after by lovers of chiptune music.

Mattel Intellivision (1980)

The *MLB* baseball game for Intellivision featured primitive play-by-play commentary—a first of its kind.

Intellivision was Mattel's first and basically only serious foray into the home console wars. The first 16-bit game console, Intellivision, offered players keypad and controller entry to interact with games. Though the product sold moderately well, its success was hobbled by difficult controllers and by announced add-ons that failed to appear or did not function as advertised. One well-known game for the Intellivision was a baseball game, *MLB*, that gave verbal feedback through synthesized voices that called strikes and outs. It had a very limited and baseball-centric vocabulary, but it was huge at the time and set the stage and standard for all sports games to come—after all, how could you have a game without a play-by-play announcer?

The Golden Age of the Arcade

It is worth mentioning that at the same time as these first home game consoles were happening, arcade video games were entering their golden age, which continued well into the 1980s. Graphic quality increased, and dedicated and sophisticated sound chips appeared. A new and innovative style of music was emerging from the simple 1s and 0s inside these machines that would go on to affect how composers would create music in the future.

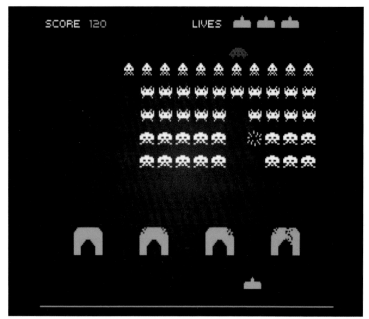

Clockwise from left: *Space Invaders* (Taito/Midway, 1978); *Donkey Kong* (Nintendo, 1981); and *Berzerk* (Stern Electronics, 1980).
Credit: Jeremy Engel.

The Invasion Begins

In 1978, Midway imported a game called *Space Invaders* from Taito. A great example of simple, effective sound design. The music for *Space Invaders* has four simple chromatic descending bass notes repeating in a loop, and is governed by a simple factor of speed related to the number of enemies present. The more enemies you kill, the faster the music would get as the remaining Invaders moved faster and got closer to the player. This was a wholly unusual and innovative concept in music that was easily implemented and yet represented a direct relationship with the game action that was not possible with traditional media at the time. The sound effects trigger over this pulsating bed a combination of laser blasts, explosions and power-ups. The overall effect is a compelling cacophony that is perfectly in tune with the gameplay.

The 1980s were the classic golden age of audio for games. Creative sound design abounded and clever folks had to use all their skills to make some very intricate stuff happen. The technology of sound was

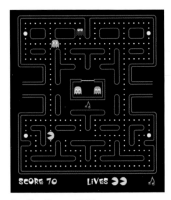

Pac-Man (Namco, 1981).

still quite basic, you might even say primitive. However, even with that being said, the sound of games really came to life for the first time in this decade, and made its way into our collective unconscious as a nation.

Later in the decade we started to see the very beginnings of MIDI (Musical Instrument Digital Interface) being used, along with mono low bit rate audio file formats. With these new innovations, the sound and scope of music was on the rise.

Pac-Man Fever

1980 also brought us the birth of a video game icon. *Pac-Man* boasts many memorable sound and music elements and truly represents a giant leap forward in overall music and sound conception. The opening ditty is one of just a few video game melodies to seriously penetrate into pop culture. One must also consider the sound of *Pac-Man* dying (blinking out), which has become a universally accepted "defeat" or "loser" sound.

Donkey Kong (1981)

The first major success of Japanese video game company Nintendo, this game featured some of the very first use of animated cutscenes to join actions and levels together into a coherent story. It introduced Jumpman, a character that was the forerunner of Mario.

Berzerk (1981)

This game featured the most recognizable voice synthesizer module of the early arcade era: "Get the humanoid!" "Intruder alert! Intruder alert!" "The humanoid must not escape!" "Chicken! Fight like a robot!"

The electronic voices and sounds from this era of games are really fun and somewhat retro to listen to today. However, they are pure classics, like a good B-movie cliché, and often mimicked and mocked in modern games.

Tempest (1981): Sound and Fury

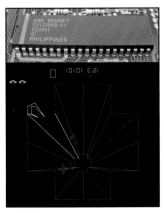

Top: Atari's POKEY audio chip. Bottom: *Tempest*, one the many Atari games that used the POKEY chip to generate sound. *Credit:* SC: Jeremy Engel, Pokey: Rod Castler.

Also in 1981, Atari's first color vector game, *Tempest*, hit the arcades, and brought with it a new next generation set of audio tools. Atari's POKEY chip was one of the first to primarily generate sound. Sound was written in a new format, Atari's own in-house SAP music format. It is no wonder that most of the well-known tunes for Atari machines used this chip and format between 1981–1987. The chip had four separate channels, and the pitch, volume, and distortion values of each could be controlled individually. Tempest used two chips, for a total of eight "voices". Atari actually released a separate soundtrack for the game, and it has the ignominious distinction of being considered to be the first stand-alone audio soundtrack in the video game industry.

Nintendo NES

With the release of the Famicom (FAMIly COMputer), which in the US was redesigned and named the NES, Nintendo rescued the console video game industry after one of its worst crashes, while at the same time creating a platform for arcade sounds and music that set the standard for video games for years to come.

The NES offered significant improvements in hardware over earlier consoles, especially in terms of video, but improvements to audio were also significant. It featured three synthesized musical voices (two pulse waves and one triangle wave) plus one noise channel multi-voice-synthesized waveforms and the ability to play PCM (pulse-code modulation) audio at 6 bits up to 33KHz (we'll talk more about what this means later in the course). This enabled composers to create primitive but reasonably full sounding music, and set the stage for composers who created those aforementioned unforgettable themes.

NES played the *Donkey Kong* titles plus a new hit, *Super Mario Bros*, an immensely popular game allegedly responsible for resurrecting the video-game industry. This console is also considered the first mature system; because the quality of its hardware approached the level in existing arcade offerings, the NES convinced a significant percentage of arcade gamers to stay home to play games, thus presaging the eventual downfall of the arcade industry.

1990s

As we move into the 1990s, cartridges become more sophisticated and hold a lot more data. There's also a new player in the game—CD-ROM. The introduction of this medium was a real game changer in the world of game audio—it opened up the doors to polyphonic MIDI, higher bit rates, and higher sample rates. Cartridges did not hold all that much information (a few megabytes for everything, actually) and that had to be shared among all the media. (The available memory for sounds for a cartridge game could be as low as 64KB!) Although it might seem like there would now be more than enough room, we will see in the next level what challenges composers and sound designers faced with the new medium.

Test your knowledge of **classic arcade games** by going over to the App, and in the main Classroom area, click on the Word Search book!

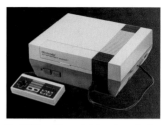

The NES from Nintendo is largely credited with rescuing the industry from the video crash of 1982, and set the standard for game consoles to come.
Credit: Evan Amos.

Koji Kondo is among the best known and loved video game composers of all time. *Credit:* Kei Noguchi.

Koji Kondo was Nintendo's first in-house composer. He composed the music for tons of popular titles but his most famous were probably *Mario Bros* in 1985 and *The Legend of Zelda* in 1986. *Super Mario Bros* was the first video game to feature constant background music. It established many conventions for game music, which survive to the present day. Speaking in an interview for Wired Magazine in March 2007, Koji states "I was just interested in the whole process . . . I wanted to create something that had never been heard before, where you'd think 'this isn't like game music at all.'" Koji continues, "First off, it had to fit the game the best, enhance the gameplay and make it more enjoyable. Not just sit there and be something that plays while you play the game, but is actually a part of the game." (Source: www.wired.com/gamelife/2007/03/vgl_koji_kondo_/).

Super Famicom

In 1991, Nintendo released the 16-bit Super Famicom in America and called the $249.95 console the Super NES (SNES). The system used a dedicated 8-bit Sony SPC700 sound chip with eight separate channels and a total sound capacity of 64KHz. You could also stream audio from the cartridge into the game, but this was hindered by the transfer rate as it streamed. All in all, this was a huge leap forward, as you could now provide music and voice-over and SFX tracks that were premixed and ready to be dropped into the game.

There's just one catch—8-bit samples sound really bad and making them sound good enough and balanced took some time, not to mention expertise.

Why 8-bit audio you ask? Good question—the answer is simple—file size. All the media in the game—programming, cutscenes, graphics, audio, etc.—have to fit within a limited space or 'budget' as it's called, based on the memory capacity of the console and the storage size on the physical medium, in this case a cartridge. Audio is often considered to be less important than great graphics or cool cutscene movies and as a result, the audio space can be quite limited.

Now with the Super NES total RAM size could be 128KB and the cartridge could hold as much as 6 Megabytes of information—yep, you heard right—6MB for the entire game!

This same story still plays out today—you still hear downsampled audio even in today's high-end console games, and for the same reasons. We'll go through the math a bit later but, for now suffice to say that the lower the sample rate and bit rate, the smaller the file.

The emergence of the Sega Genesis ignited a well-known console war between them and Nintendo for dominance of the market. *Credit:* Evan Amos.

Sega Genesis

Sega, a Japanese and American maker of arcade games, got into the console business around the same time as Nintendo, and experienced moderate success until the debut of the Genesis (also called the Sega Mega Drive in Japan) in 1988, before the SNES came out. The Genesis, similar in some ways to the SNES, featured even less memory capacity with total of 64KB of RAM and only 8KB of dedicated sound RAM. Still, sound quality wise, it represented a significant step up, as it featured a Yamaha FM chip with some built-in sounds, and 6 stereo audio channels.

The Sega CD was an add-on to the Genesis Console, though it later came bundled together. This combination created one of the first consoles to feature CD-ROM media, greatly enhancing audio and musical content in addition to higher quality graphics and animations.
Credit: Evan Amos.

Sega CD Released

In 1992, another huge advance took place when Sega released the $299 Sega CD system. The console itself was very similar to the Genesis in power, but the big difference was the inclusion of a 500 MB **CD-ROM** disc. This was a huge jump in storage capacity and allowed developers to add high-end graphics, and of course high-end sound if desired. The SEGA CD also included a total of 18 sound channels, a sample rate of 44.1 KHz and separate audio outputs for connecting to a household stereo system. All this along with the FM General MIDI-compatible chip set made for a lot of new sonic possibilities.

A Sega CD game of this period typically might have a series of fully produced opening cutscenes, multiple levels of gameplay with a background MIDI score, some number of 16-bit, stereo audio tracks (as much as the producer would allow, depending on sound budget), hundreds if not thousands of individual sound effects, and many many lines of voice-over. You can see that this is a gigantic improvement on the 3-voice NES! All this audio from these various sources had to be mixed and blended together to sound good in the game, which was no small task.

N64 and Game Cube

Nintendo, in a heated competition with Sega for dominance of the home console market, continued to update its game machines throughout the years. First in 1996 with the Nintendo 64, then in 2001 with the Gamecube. The 64 was a beefed-up, cartridge-based 64-bit system and the Cube was optical disc based. Both had a huge selection of games and audio technology was getting better and making it possible to include more music, sound effects and voice-over than ever before.

A collection of early computers. Clockwise from top: Commodore C64; Macintosh; Atari 1040ST; and the innovative Amiga. Of these computers, only the Mac and PC survived.

The Rise of Home Computers

At the same time as the console wars were heating up, PC games were also turning a corner. Although they developed somewhat concurrently with the console (debuting just between the 2600 and the NES), and there were popular games (especially in the adventure genre) the use of computers for gaming did not achieve significant momentum until the 1990s when CD-ROM technology improved graphic quality tremendously, and dedicated sound cards could improve the immersive qualities of the gaming experience.

The Commodore 64 (1982)

The Commodore 64 was released to the public in August of 1982 with a BASIC (Beginner's All-purpose Symbolic Instruction Code) programming environment. Its graphic and sound capabilities, advanced for the time, were similar to those on the lesser known ColecoVision console.

Because the Commodore 64 used the same game-controller ports popularized by the Atari 2600, gamers could use their old joysticks with their new computers. The Commodore 64 became the most popular home computer of its day in the United States and many other countries, and it remains the top-selling single computer model of all time internationally.

Apple Macintosh (1984)

The Apple Macintosh was the first (somewhat) inexpensive computer featuring a graphical user interface (GUI), which ran on top of the operating system. The Macintosh also featured the innovation of the mouse as a device for input and navigation. Though comparatively inexpensive, the machine remained out of reach of the pockets of most of the public. It found popularity in schools, with creative artists, and in desktop-publishing environments.

Atari ST (1984)

The ST (short for sixteen and thirty-two) featured a GUI system called GEM, and was popular with composers in its day, since it featured a MIDI interface and later offered 8-bit stereo-sound playback.

Test your knowledge of Game Platforms by going over to the App, and in the main Classroom area, click on the Word Search book!

Commodore Amiga (1985)

The Amiga was a computer ahead of its time that unfortunately never caught on outside of a small dedicated market segment. It featured significantly better display at 4096 colors, could produce 8-bit stereo audio, and also run many applications at the same time.

IBM PC (1981)

Although the development of the PC, originally by IBM, started earlier than many of these machines, its effects are still being felt today in the gaming world. The practice of PC 'cloning' by other overseas makers, combined with the emergence of Microsoft as a provider of operating systems, propelled the PC to preeminence in the business world. At that time the platform was initially rarely used for gaming because it had low graphics performance and no sound, and this continued throughout most of the 1980s.

However, the emergence of third-party producers of hardware such as enhanced video and sound cards began to level the playing field in comparison with dedicated consoles. By the late 1990s, due to this high performing hardware, PC games were squeezing out arcades and competing neck-and-neck for market share with consoles.

The Playstation consoles. Clockwise from top: Playstation One; Playstation 2 (thin version); Playstation 2 (original version); Playstation 3; Playstation 4, the newest console (2013–present).

Sony Playstation

In 1995 Sony got in the game with the 32-bit PlayStation, at a price of $299. The 24-channel sound chip in the Playstation provided CD-quality stereo sound plus built-in support for digital effects such as reverb and delay. The added storage, speed and memory really gave composers and designers some room to work. The Playstation allocated greater memory for audio storage, allowing for more realistic sounding samples. Sony released the Playstation 2 in 2000, and then the Playstation 3 in 2006. The Playstation 3, for example, featured the ability to handle hundreds of sounds simultaneously on the CPU, along with a maximum of 12 continuous audio streams. Output was available via HDMI with eight channels of audio, surround sound and Stereo/Dolby Digital/DTS. The latest entry, the Playstation 4, has once again upped the ante, featuring an 8 core processor and a dedicated sound processing chip with the ability to decompress hundreds of MP3 audio streams at one time.

Voyeur, a mystery adventure game released in 1993 by Philips Interactive, featured one of the first orchestral soundtracks.

Released in 1993 for the short-lived Philips Interactive system, the mystery/adventure game *Voyeur* was one of the first to feature high quality full motion video, but also has the distinction of being one of the first game titles to use a full orchestral score, composed by Garry

31

Schyman, who later become well-known for his work on games like *Dante's Inferno* and the *BioShock* series (most recently with *BioShock Infinite* released in 2013).

2000s

As we entered the 2000s and the current new millennium, transfer speeds increased dramatically. CD-ROM, DVD and these higher streaming rates again led to higher bit rate and higher sample rate audio in games.

The different Xboxes. Left to right: Xbox One (2013); the newest console; the original Xbox (2001); and Xbox 360 (2005), which was the first to feature the unique camera-based sensor, the Kinect, involving body movement as the controller. *Credit:* Evan Amos, Frederik Hermann.

Nintendo's revolutionary Wii (2006) and the Wii U (2012) which feature an innovative controller. *Credit:* Evan Amos, Takimata.

Microsoft Xbox

In 2001, Microsoft decided to capitalize on their expertise in PC gaming by releasing the Xbox. The Xbox console had a lot of firepower, and has continued to increase its capacity over the years. The Xbox 360 featured multi-channel surround sound output, 48KHz 16-bit audio, 320 independent decompression channels, 32-bit audio processing, and over 256 separate audio channels! The recently released 8-core Xbox One also has a dedicated audio processor called SHAPE (Scalable Hardware Audio Processing Engine) with three dedicated audio processors! Working together, SHAPE provides 512 compressed XMA audio voices, 128 dedicated mix voices, over 2000 simple filters (assignable to hardware or virtual voices) and 512 EQ/Compressor effects.

Nintendo Wii

In 2006, Nintendo released the Wii. The console was a huge hit, due to its focus on motion controllers and interactive user experiences. The Wii features a dedicated audio processor, 64 voices, 44.1 and 48KHz sample rates, 16-bit resolution, and it uses 512MB of shared memory. Plus a speaker in the hand controller! The newest addition to the Wii family is the Wii U. Featuring a large touchscreen controller, it supports HD video output. Audio-wise, the dedicated processor is still there, but beefed up a bit to handle 64+ surround audio channels instead of stereo like the original Wii.

Conclusion

So as you can see, the story of sound in the history of games is the story of innovative companies and artists working on next-generation technologies. From the silent era to the modern amalgam of formats, sound for games has traveled in leaps and bounds. As we move to the next level, we'll touch on many of the issues and challenges that have helped to develop many of the current conventions that are used in creating and implementing sound into games.

The Interactive Quiz for this Level is available in the App. In the main Classroom, click on the Quiz book to test your knowledge!

My Non-Linear Life
Audio For Interactive Environments

Learning Outcomes:
Linear vs non-linear—the nuts and bolts of why games are different from film/TV ·
Understand how interactivity affects audio design ·
Some of the major technical developments in game audio history ·

In this level, we'll look at these and many more such challenges that forced game audio developers to devise solutions to the unique difficulties they faced. We'll also get familiar with a few concepts and terminologies that will help us going forward.

There are a few basics we need to get out of the way first, having to do with the basic nature of how digital audio works. This information is always front and center in the mind of the video game sound person, because of the relationship of file size and fidelity to the space allowed in the game, as well as how efficiently these sounds can be triggered.

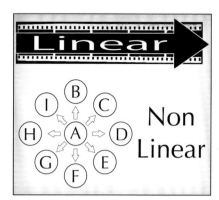

The top image shows a linear concept, similar to film, TV or video. All events must be in a particular order, and the order cannot be changed. The bottom image shows a non-linear concept where possibilities can change from one moment to the next.

35

CHALLENGES OF INTERACTIVE MEDIA

Now that we've laid out a rough timeline of the significant events in game audio in the last level, what are the chief challenges a game audio person must face in designing sounds for this new medium? Well, the biggest difference is that game audio is primarily non-linear in nature. So what does that mean?

To understand this situation more fully let's consider a linear medium like film or television. The key word for this situation is predictability. In a film, if a character goes into the dark spooky castle and opens the door at 13 minutes and 22 seconds, you can easily create or obtain a sound of a creaking door and place it on the timeline in your favorite DAW (Digital Audio Workstation) at that exact point. Once you synchronize it correctly with the film itself, it will always play at the same time. In other words, it's predictable—you know exactly when it will happen.

Now imagine watching this same film, only each time you watch it, the character goes into the house at different times. This is a prime example of the unpredictability and indeterminacy inherent in games. How could you successfully create sounds for a medium in which you don't know when in time a particular action is going to happen? How can you create a way to trigger them reliably?

The answer in this case, is that largely, you need to throw away using time as a basis for organizing these sounds and concentrate on the actions in the movie itself. Let's think of our spooky house situation from the angle of the action involved. So at some point, the character is going to come up to the house and open the door. It doesn't matter when. So let's list it as an action like this:

Action #001 Spooky Door Opening → Play 'spookydoor.wav'

Now we've defined our action—but how do we trigger it? In a movie, we may be out of luck, but fortunately in the game there's already something that's going to cause the door to move. Most likely this will be some kind of animation code. So we then hook up the code that triggers the animation of the door with the sound of a creaky door and voila! Instant sync—whenever the character opens the door the sound will play.

However, this shift in thinking requires that each sound in the game exists as a separate item. We mostly can't use a mix of the sound effects and music anymore, except in certain situations. Everything has to be independently mixed and mastered separately. Furthermore, we have to be really organized with all of these audio files (for huge AAA adventure games there can be hundreds of thousands of files!) so that the programmer knows what to do with these assets in the game.

It also means that how the audio is triggered in a game is intimately tied up with how the game is designed, and each game is a complete universe unto itself. It's got its own sets of rules and regulations and rules for emergent behavior and interactivity, and any change in terms of game design can significantly affect how the sounds are triggered.

Digital Sampling Basics

Everybody should be familiar to at least some extent with the principles behind digital sampling. Essentially it's very close to the process used for film. In that situation a camera takes a certain amount of pictures, or frames, in a second, of some kind of action. When all of these frames are run back, the result fools the eye into believing that smooth motion is taking place. In digital audio the process is similar but much faster than in movies, and we need to take a lot more 'pictures' to fool the ear than the eye.

Go to the Main Classroom in the App, and click on the video screen to learn more about linear vs non-linear media and adaptive audio.

Pulse-Code Modulation (PCM)

This method of representing analog signals in digital form is the basis of how data for uncompressed audio is encoded. The method uses sampling of the analog signal level at a specific interval, and each sample is converted to a digital value. PCM includes all uncompressed audio files of any kind like WAV and AIFF, or media encoded on CDs, DVDs, and Blu-Ray. Since the data is represented in a single linear stream it's often referred to as Linear PCM or LPCM.

There are two specific characteristics that define how PCM data is encoded. The **sample rate** is effectively the number of audio pictures taken per second. The higher the sampling rate, the higher the quality of audio, but also the larger the file size. Sampling is measured in hertz, or cycles per second, and is usually found in the tens of thousands range. For example, CD-quality audio (often referred to as '44.1') is at 44,100 samples per second. This is commonly represented as 44.1KHz or kilohertz.

Now the human ear can technically hear from about 20Hz all the way up to 20KHz. So why such a high rate? There's a lot of mathematical reasons for this but the most important is that we need at least two samples to describe any frequency. So this means that the highest frequency we can hear from a sample rate of 44.1KHz is half of it—in this case 22.05KHz— just about where our ears stop hearing anyway. This is called the Nyquist frequency.

The next important thing to be concerned about here is **bit resolution** or **bit depth**. This governs how wide a range of volume each sample has. Here again, more bits = better fidelity, but it also means larger file size. There is a lot of binary math here, but to simplify the situation each bit of

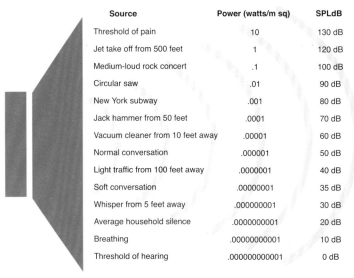

Source	Power (watts/m sq)	SPLdB
Threshold of pain	10	130 dB
Jet take off from 500 feet	1	120 dB
Medium-loud rock concert	.1	100 dB
Circular saw	.01	90 dB
New York subway	.001	80 dB
Jack hammer from 50 feet	.0001	70 dB
Vacuum cleaner from 10 feet away	.00001	60 dB
Normal conversation	.000001	50 dB
Light traffic from 100 feet away	.0000001	40 dB
Soft conversation	.00000001	35 dB
Whisper from 5 feet away	.000000001	30 dB
Average household silence	.0000000001	20 dB
Breathing	.00000000001	10 dB
Threshold of hearing	.000000000001	0 dB

Increasing intensity of a variety of common sounds in decibels, from near total silence to extremely loud. Also note the increase in power at each of these levels.

resolution in a sample is equal to about 6dB (decibels) of dynamic range. We can't explain what decibels are, except to say you should really know how decibels work if you don't already.

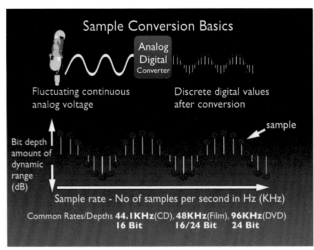

Diagram showing basic analog to digital audio conversion. The larger the sample rate and bit depth, the larger the resulting file.

Adding more bits gives us a larger difference between our quietest volume and our loudest volume. A rule of thumb is that around 90–100dB is commonly associated with digital media. CD is recorded at 16-bit, so multiplying 6×16 gets us 96dB, roughly the difference between a pin drop and a jet plane going by your ear. DVD audio is recorded at 24-bit, which is 144dB.

There are many different compression types used in games depending on the hardware platform, but probably the most popular one out there is the MP3 codec. Apple has gravitated towards the AAC codec, while many games use the more recently developed Ogg Vorbis (OGG) codec, due to its open source nature.

AUDIO COMPRESSION

While you might be familiar with term 'compression' as it's used in the audio industry, we are specifically referring to data compression here—that is, compression whose purpose it is to reduce the size of the file. How compression works is a pretty complex topic, but each type of file compression uses a special piece of code to encode (compress) the file into this format, and another piece of code is required to decode (decompress) the file and play it back. The algorithm for encoding and decoding is referred to as a **codec**, short for COmpression/DECompression, and a computer must have the proper codec to play back these encoded files. Although such compressed files often use the same bit depth as uncompressed files, they are considered a **lossy** format, which means they will lose data permanently compared to the original uncompressed file.

Besides the codec type and bit depth, the main characteristic that determines quality in a compressed file is the **bit rate**, usually measured in kilobits per second (Kbps). Again, the same rules apply here. The higher the bit rate, the higher the quality, and the larger the file. 128Kbps is generally considered minimum decent quality for music or ambiences, while lower quality voice or sounds can be found at lesser bit rates.

FM Synthesis

In frequency modulation synthesis (or FM synthesis), the timbre of simple waveform (usually a sine wave) called a carrier, is changed by modulating it with another waveform in the audio range (higher than 20Hz). The result is a complex waveform with a different tone. Video-game developers used FM synthesis in the past because the sounds created by FM synthesis took up less space than those created through PCM. Nowadays FM synthesis is commonly found in modern DAWs as a plug-in. The sound is also considered 'retro' and is still used in certain specialized 'tracker' applications to reproduce the sound of a well-loved era of gaming.

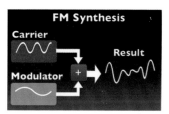

A simplification of FM Synthesis, originally developed by John Chowning at Stanford, and patented by Yamaha.

MIDI

The Musical Instrument Digital Interface, or MIDI, is one the most innovative and far reaching standards developed in the last 30 years and is still heavily in use today. It is an industry protocol enabling different manufacturers to control and trigger events (musical or otherwise) by sending messages back and forth on a serial connection. Keep in mind MIDI isn't audio but it can certainly control audio.

Games use MIDI like a player-piano roll to trigger sounds and music passages. When used in conjunction with FM synthesis, for example, MIDI can trigger a significant amount of music and sound for very little file size.

A MIDI interface and MIDI cables. MIDI data can also be used internally and transmitted wirelessly.
Credit: Jeremy Engel.

Recently, MIDI achieved industry recognition by winning a technical Grammy. Dave Smith, the polyphonic synthesizer pioneer, and Ikutaro Kakehashi, a Yamaha engineer, were both honored for the creation of this amazing language spoken by synthesizers, samplers, drum machines, computers, sequencers and much much more, that enabled digital music to advance to never-before-seen levels of sophistication.

In the last level, we concentrated on the technology of sound for games as it developed over a 40-year span. Now let's take a look at some of the creative uses of these formats as they pertain to the craft of game audio design.

EARLY CONSOLE AND ARCADE GAME DEVELOPMENT CHALLENGES

Many fundamental sound-design concepts and iconic sound effects were developed in this time period. The effort of making these sounds trigger within the game was no easy task. Early video-game designers used raw programming of computer chips to create music, sound effects, and even voice-overs. These chips generated complex waveforms that sent tones to speakers in real time.

Programming the sounds and music for these was really just like that—programming. There were literally no tools in the mid-to-late 1970s that could enable anyone without significant computer coding expertise to create music for these games. There was no way to record musical performances into a computer—even MIDI did not exist yet! Everything had to be painstakingly entered into the cartridge's or arcade board's chip one sound at a time, and then 'burned' into the EEPROM, a primitive programmable ROM chip. Many of these chips were coded by programmers who knew next to nothing about sound or music. Unfortunately, even though the tools for creating sounds and triggering music have been largely simplified, such that today's composers and designers can provide these assets for games, the practice of using programmers with no audio or music experience continues today, especially in smaller game companies with limited budgets.

CONSOLE AND ARCADE WORKFLOW IMPROVEMENTS AND CHALLENGES

As game platforms continued to develop in sophistication, console hardware was finally able to play more than one note at a time—3 or 4 notes with the NES, and increasingly more notes with subsequent models and makers. The tools for creation of this music got more streamlined, such that it didn't require a computer science degree to understand how to enter in the music or create the effects.

Creative sound design abounded, as clever folks used their skills to produce intricate results. The technology of sound remained quite basic, even primitive. Even so, from games that talked to games that produced top-10 radio hits, sound in games came to life for the first time, making its way into the collective unconscious.

The result of this was that finally game composers like Nobuo Uematsu, Koji Kondo, etc., could finally compose really timeless and unforgettable themes, albeit with significant restrictions. See sidebar for Nobuo's take on the situation.

The sounds of this early eighties game sound were still being generated by using simple synthesizer waveforms like triangles, pulse waves and noise generators. Filters and EQs didn't exist at the time, which meant that game music had an in-your-face music quality that didn't allow for a lot of subtlety. Fading the audio or music up and down smoothly was largely impossible, due to the small number of assignable volume levels available. Looping was common in music for audio data space and code considerations (the 'audio budget') as well as the aforementioned need to loop because of the indeterminacy in the game itself.

If you were making sound effects for these games, you mostly had to use the waveforms and get very creative with how you used them. Many effects such as the familiar *Super Mario Bros* power-up sound effect to make Mario bigger are just incredibly sped-up versions of common arpeggiations on chords using pitched waveforms. Other effects mix both noise and pitched sounds to get a more convincing result. In fact the sound design part was really the place where artists could get more creative, since music was limited in many respects, in that it was expected to create normal melodies and rhythms.

The arcade world had similar situations that enabled composers and sound designers to be less technical wizards, especially after Atari's development of the POKEY chip and the SAP format, but while the sound

Nobuo Uematsu

"The NES only had three tracks, and each of their sounds were very unique. I had to focus on the melody itself and think about how each chord will move the audience. I struggled to produce originality in the same three tones, just like any composer from that period. It's amazing to listen to how each of us— Konami composers, Koichi Sugiyama, and Namco composers—had totally different creations by using the same three instruments. There was an originality in 'Game Music' back then."

quality of arcades versus consoles was clearly superior in favor of arcade games, by the end of the eighties, the distance was closing fast.

Although arcade games had short, jaunty music themes, because of the action-oriented nature and general lack of character development, it tended to be the sound design that became well known, and passed into the cultural language, such as the *Pac-Man* dying sound that we mentioned before. Add to that memorable sounds from games like *Defender*, *Joust*, *Tempest*, and many many others.

FM Emerges, MIDI Helps Out Too

Earlier we talked about the basics of FM synthesis. Although FM synthesizers could produce really innovative sounds and effects, in game consoles they showed up as chips by Yamaha (who purchased the technology from the inventors, John Chowning and Max Mathews) with a number of preset sounds that tried to emulate acoustic instruments. FM was better than analog synthesis at modeling plucking or striking such as for mallet instruments, harps and electric pianos. However, it too came with a lot of limitations—thin, unrealistic sound, no filtering (although adjustment of algorithms and levels under the hood could produce variations in timbre). Volume changes and fades were potentially more possible, although game developers initially only rarely used them.

Since MIDI was introduced in 1982 and debuted first in the Yamaha DX-7 FM synthesizer, the association of MIDI with FM instruments has been an ongoing phenomenon. In game consoles it seems to have started with the Yamaha YM2612 FM chip, a six voice FM chip first found in the Sega Genesis console. This chip could be programmed to play via the game's memory via MIDI and could even use patch data from compatible Yamaha FM synthesizers to create the sounds. This meant that composers could create or use particular patches they liked on their FM synths, and transfer it over to the sound card via MIDI System Exclusive messaging, and the game would use the patch data to play its sounds in the game. Nifty! The early game consoles like the Sega Genesis even featured stereo sound, though this was often distorted and improved only later.

Why Use MIDI?

The answer, once again is—file size! MIDI files are tiny, since they contain no sound—MIDI is just a series of coded commands that tells sound how to play. So, if your sounds are small and compact, you can create a tremendous amount of music and sound for very little footprint. Although MIDI in games is somewhat less used, especially at the AAA level, it still plays a huge role in the creation of the media itself.

DIGITAL AUDIO ENTERS THE PICTURE

Although extremely primitive versions of digitized sound in games had been used since the beginning of the 1980s, putting sampled sound into a game as a regular feature did not come fully into practice until early in the next decade.

Since one of the very first game titles to use any digitized audio was a sports game, it's probably not surprising that the first game to use continuous play-by-play commentary was also a sports title: *Joe Montana II Sports Talk Football* for the Sega Genesis. Previous games featured the occasional synthesized voice or short sample, but *Sports Talk* was the first game featuring an announcer who described the action as it happened.

One catch was the quality; 8-bit samples sounded grainy and distorted. Improving sound quality (relatively) and balance required time and expertise. The more samples that were triggered simultaneously, the more background noise the player heard.

Understanding the chart below is vital. . . .

Another thing to understand about this time period—there were no audio-compression schemes commonly available like MP3 that could run on consoles, much less arcades, and their common use in games wasn't going to be for almost another decade.

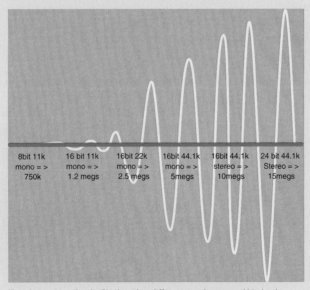

| 8bit 11k mono = > 750k | 16 bit 11k mono = > 1.2 megs | 16bit 22k mono = > 2.5 megs | 16bit 44.1k mono = > 5megs | 16bit 44.1k stereo = > 10megs | 24 bit 44.1k Stereo = > 15megs |

The relative sizes of audio files based on different sample rates and bit depths. Before widely available compression technology, sound designers would have to use lower sample rates/bit depths in order to keep file sizes small, with a corresponding decrease in audio quality as a result. Measurements based on a 1-minute stereo file.

The 8-Bit 'Secret Sauce'?

Many audio houses at this time started developing their own special techniques for converting audio from high quality (16-bit, 44.1KHz) to low (8-bit, 11KHz) using lot of fancy (and expensive) digital compression and noise reduction tools. It took time and patience, but you could actually make 8-bit files sound a bit better (relative term) by doing this. The secret was in the sauce and each audio developer had their own recipe that they swore blew away the competition. Sound effects were the easiest, but voice-over posed the biggest challenge and games in the 1990s started to use a lot of voice-over.

Also notice the quality of the music in *Sports Talk*. What you are hearing is a small MIDI file that triggers the YM2612 chip. Besides using the FM patches from the synths, the chip is also compatible with what became known as General MIDI. GM, as it's called, is a way of ensuring that every MIDI device potentially has the exact same basic sounds at a particular setting. For example, drums would always appear on Channel 10. Program number 001 on every musical channel (except Channel 10) would play a piano sound. This enabled composers to try to make their soundtracks sound the same way on different platforms. However, hardware differences of sound engines or different chips caused MIDI to garner a certain reputation over the years for 'sounding bad'. But in fact, this is completely false as MIDI sounds like nothing at all. If a capable sound chip was used by a

CD-ROM SAVES THE DAY?

We mentioned previously that the invention and adoption of CD-ROM was a huge advance for games and game audio. Remember that up to this point we had been dealing with a complete game budget somewhere around 6MB. Now suddenly you have a lot more space (650MB to be exact) to store information of all kinds. That's over 100 times the space of a typical console game!

Although at first glance it would seem like a huge improvement with lots more room for music and audio assets, the game world did not cater to sound designers' wishes. Although there was definitely more room than before, higher-end graphics and animations took a lot of that space away. There was another catch that hobbled game composers and sound designers; early CD-ROM drives were only one speed and the transfer speeds were a huge issue and often incurred significant delays in streaming that information into the game environment, again forcing the sound designer/composer into compensating for this situation. Later CD-ROM models had higher transfer speeds, easing this situation. Later consoles featured significantly more sound capabilities as well, and in general, specs were moving up. Increased memory, faster streaming, and additional storage capacity anticipated the move to DVD storage.

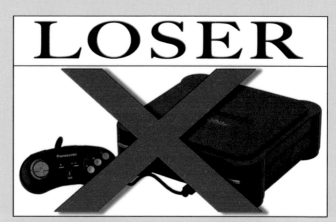

The 3DO console, introduced in 1993, was a notable victim of the volatile game industry. Advanced for its time, it was also massively overpriced and could not compete with the cheaper Nintendo and Sega consoles. The company collapsed after three years of dismal sales.
Credit: Jeremy Engel.

Although a few brands besides Sega and Nintendo tried compete in this space, such as Panasonic with its 3DO system, they could not compete on the same level and soon exited the market.

PC GAMING COMES OF AGE

Although the PC was definitely established as a gaming platform, and its market share increased due to the interest in adventure games, the development of games for PCs was stuck in a low gear of sorts until CD-ROM came around in the 1990s. Very quickly after its introduction, however, developers saw the potential in it and the modern multimedia movement ascended to another level of sophistication.

Once again, though, there was a catch. We already outlined issues that sound and music folks faced with CD-ROM, but with the PC there were numerous models of PCs (and at that time, Macs and even Mac clones) each with different hardware and software drivers. Due to this, the job of making music and sound work correctly in this patchwork world was often fraught with dangers of inconsistency and interoperability.

well-versed composer, familiar with its limitations, the results could be quite pleasing. It was when you tried to create the same sound on PCs that the difficulties would arise, as we shall see later on.

Some companies making games had no idea how much audio they could fit on the media itself. Others wanted music but did not know how to trigger it in the game. Many PCs even shipped without sound cards, and some of the ones that did have cards had no sounds or drivers installed on them! And even though standards like General MIDI helped establish which types of sounds or effects could be found at particular MIDI settings, there was no subsequent uniformity to the banks of sounds. Each sound device manufacturer would create their version of a piano, bass, or drumset sound, and the more esoteric sounds like effects could be wildly inconsistent. As a result, music and sound effects often sounded different from machine to machine.

Frustrated with the situation, the audio community united to push for audio standards such as DLS (Downloadable Sounds), and 3D audio. In 1992, Roland Corporation released the first General MIDI-compatible audio card for the PC.

This card gave the home user something similar to what audio developers used. Over the next 15 or so years, 3D sound for games (also called spatial audio) became popular and standardized. Pushed forward by increasingly interactive music and sound design, new standards and tools were developed. Surround-sound playback and other mixing and mastering features were added to the hardware and software capabilities of many game engines.

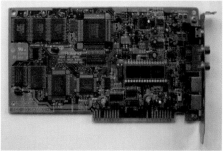

The Roland SCC-1 was the first General MIDI soundcard for the PC, and offered comparable high-level audio and musical performance as the separate SC-55 SoundCanvas module. *Credit:* Austriacus.

Game Audio in the Modern Age of Games and Consoles

As we look at the next batch of games and consoles, we enter the modern age of the big three competing consoles. Companies such as Electronic Arts, Activision Blizzard, and Capcom have acquired multiple development studios and release games in multiple formats. Teams of audio designers and composers work both in-house and as contractors to create an array of music and sounds.

You learned in the previous module that, in the San Francisco Bay Area, the merger of Silicon Valley and Hollywood was referred to as 'Siliwood.' As production values rose, so did the amount of money spent on games and interactive media. In many games of this period, money was spent on elaborate cutscenes, designed to push the story line along in between gameplay. This was a result of the increased storage capacity of the CD-ROM format, and game designers wanted to take advantage of this increased capacity to expand the narrative aspects of gaming.

So you might be asking yourself "Why is it important that I know all of this ancient history? What's so important about things like sample formats and file size restrictions that I need to know all about 8-bit audio and MIDI?"

Well for one reason, it's fun and informative to know about the past, and another is that it is seriously applicable today! Remember that old quote "Those who do not remember history are doomed to repeat it."

Modern workflow in games still deals with many of the same challenges experiences by sound designers in the past. Incompatible formats, multiple compression schemes, variable transfer speeds and streaming problems all demand creative solutions and thoughtful designers who understand modern day systems. This problem is not likely to go away soon, because the industry is always innovating. For example, Google's Android OS is just now being used in low-level consoles (the Ouya for example), and the ability of Android to do much of anything advanced in audio is somewhat limited. Anyone designing for these devices must take into account the sound capabilities of the various platforms, and this means understanding limitations and working around them. Let's say someone wanted to release a game for iOS as well as Android. Did you know that iOS doesn't support Ogg Vorbis files? And that MP3s created by most applications won't seamlessly loop? You see, even in the twenty-first century, inconsistencies abound in the wacky world of sound for games.

Middleware

Technologically speaking, things in games got so good for sound artists that around 2000, new pieces of software called **middleware** started cropping up. The first middleware engines for audio were around throughout the

1990s and even beforehand. These were custom made and proprietary tools; game companies kept the software in-house for their own use. In many cases, middleware was developed by audio folks and programmers working together to solve workflow issues and smooth out production cycles. As these tools became sought after, third-party developers started to produce them and make them available to the general public.

Why was middleware needed? Well, music and sound designers and programmers developed middleware so that the designers and composers could gain more control over how their audio was used in games. Programs such as FMOD, Wwise, Miles, and xACT provide graphical interfaces and suites of interactive audio tools directly to music and sound professionals. Middleware is based on the idea that the video game is an interactive medium, so all audio elements within the game should be interactive as well.

Just for fun, let's set the clock around 2002. We've got high-end consoles like the Playstation 2 and the Microsoft Xbox that feature staggeringly

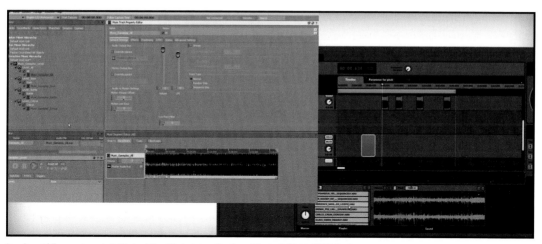

Popular middleware Apps. Left: Wwise (WaveWorks Interactive Sound Engine). Right: FMOD Studio, newest version of FMOD.
Credit: Jeremy Engel.

impressive graphics, fast CDs and DVDs streaming multiple high quality audio and music tracks. Composers and sound designers working for AAA studios create their assets in Digital Audio Workstations and integrate these assets using custom tools written for them by in-house programmers. The workflow is demanding, but the act of creation seemingly comes with little regard for limitations, and basically, the sky's the limit. Sounds like a cool situation, right?

Well around that same time (actually a few years before), something called the Internet, or more specifically the World Wide Web, became a very interesting place for gaming. Folks had these things called modems that they would use to access the Web. At first, internet connections were not so fast, but over time they became much faster and are getting faster all the time. You could potentially play a game on your PC without having to put a CD, DVD, or any physical media into your machine, and the software could be downloaded directly to your computer, via the Internet.

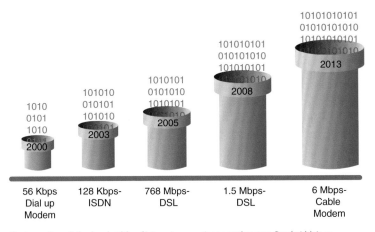

| 56 Kbps
Dial up
Modem | 128 Kbps-
ISDN | 768 Mbps-
DSL | 1.5 Mbps-
DSL | 6 Mbps-
Cable
Modem |

The increasing relative bandwidths of Internet connections over the years. Bandwidth is an extremely important criterion for creating sounds for any web-based games. Lower bandwidth means correspondingly lower audio quality, while higher bandwidth gives much better quality, but can create issues on older and slower connections.

About this time, a little program called Flash made by Macromedia (and then purchased by Adobe later on) was catching on as a platform for game development.

The first Internet games that used Flash had on average one piece of music around 20 to 30 seconds in length, three to 10 sound effects and a handful of voice-over lines, all of which had to fit in the game at around 30–50KB. Sound familiar. . . ?

Flash was able to efficiently compress its graphic and sound data into a stream that ordinary users could download without too much trouble. If Flash was limited to triggering regular PCM audio, this could have been a problem—even a deal killer, as the PCM audio could potentially result in huge download times. To get around these limitations, Flash used a funny little compression scheme that not many game audio folks knew about at the time called MP3 (of course music MP3s were tremendously common in the music file sharing community). The use of MP3 compression within Flash made for a fairly straightforward audio workflow.

There was no need to compress files ahead of time and all the audio assets could be created in a typical DAW (Digital Audio Workstation— like Pro Tools or Logic) at CD quality or higher. Then once the sound was imported into the Flash library, various compression schemes were available to bring the size of these files into line with the speed of the user's internet connection. No more worrying about downsampling and no more valiant attempts at trying to make low bit rate audio sound good. That was the upside—the downside is that Flash could not trigger MIDI files and had no ability to add reverb or equalization to the sound after it had been created—everything had to be baked into the audio file. Again, one step forward and two steps back.

Now, as the years went on and bandwidth increased in speed with DSL, Cable Modem and T1 lines, downloadable games started to get a lot more complex. You could still trigger PCM audio with the aforementioned limitations, or use MP3 (the more common approach) but, the number of channels available grew to eight or more and the quality of the MP3 compression also increased from 8 or 16Kbps to as much as 192Kbps, which is pretty much CD quality. Nowadays, it is not unusual to find downloadable games with as much as 20MB of audio in them, the total downloads for the entire game sometimes over 100MB. As small as that might seem, you just might be surprised how much rich audio content you can fit into a game this size by utilizing these new compression technologies.

Early cell phones had extremely low bandwidth and different standards for each device. Some had little FM music players on board, some didn't. There were a ton of different handsets on the market, all from different carriers and manufacturers, though lately the smartphone has dominated with fewer manufacturers. Still all of these devices have different audio specs. What a nightmare. Seriously, there are still over 100 different audio formats and they all have special converters and special programs for creating them. Some games even ship, yes, you guessed it, with no sounds at all. . . !

Now, the iPhone and iPad along with Android devices are changing the playing field for Social, mobile games and tablets. With these games there is a fair amount of rich media, and most importantly, standard development platforms. These devices can run natively within their respective OSs, or as Flash or HTML5-based Apps (with or without the browser) and are helping to define a new generation of touch-based gaming that has fantastic new sound potential. A whole host of new game development platforms are springing up, accessible to a large and increasingly diverse base. However, as mentioned before, this brave new world is filled with various pitfalls for the unwary audio developer who is unprepared for a whole host of new audio challenges.

Unity 3D is among the latest game engines to appear and features a fairly robust set of audio features. In fact, the Application that accompanies this book is developed in Unity3D.

Handheld games are also competing on the market. The Nintendo DS and PSP and Vita all feature lots of great games, along with some interesting audio capabilities. Powered by the Virtual Mobile Engine, the PSP features built-in stereo playback, surround sound support with headphones, a GM-compatible synthesizer, audio EQ, playback compression and a built-in microphone for interesting interactive audio capabilities. There has been more than one game that asks the user to blow or speak into the microphone in order to make something happen in the game. If you listen to these games, they sound very similar to some of the original golden age games of the early 1980s. No wonder, as the audio developers once again must learn how to make sound magic happen in less than 200KB.

Conclusion
The More Things Change. . .

As you can see, the sound for games is ever changing and morphing; as this book goes to press, HTML5 and other formats are boldly moving into the future. Flash, a long-time and well-used stalwart of the online gaming industry, may be on its last legs, and no one really knows which platforms will be around in five years. These rapidly shifting tides in the game industry can make you seasick, but are common and present opportunities for entrepreneurially minded audio folks. One thing is certain—as audio professionals in games, it is part of our job to understand the capabilities of these new formats. We must be technical evangelists to one degree or another, because our jobs depend on it. After all, how can you possibly create the soundtrack for the next mega cult hit without knowing what the hardware and software can do for you?

The Interactive Quiz for this Level is available in the App. In the main Classroom, click on the Quiz book to test your knowledge!

x F P S O E A
F L P U M V D
A F U W M M V
O Y B R S U E
J T X C S W N
H R E U S R T
V Z M R E U
T A E B U Q R

What Is Hip?
Styles and Genres—Welcome to Acronym Hell

Learning Outcomes:
Comprehend gameplay structure and interactive design •
Gain familiarity with game styles and genres •
Understand the audio challenges faced by professionals •

The Flavor Pill

Games come in all kinds of flavors and forms, and part of your job as a game audio professional is understanding these forms. How you create sounds for an MMO may be very different from the way you'd work with an RTS game or a FPS or TPS game. Wait, you don't know what all those acronyms mean? Well, welcome to Acronym Hell . . .

Seriously though—as audio experts, it is crucial for us to understand the basic gameplay mechanics for each of these genres. Another thing to keep in mind—game mechanics and genres are constantly in flux and many designers will often combine elements of several of these types of gameplay. If the game sells well, it can sometimes become a genre or style by itself that can then be copied or adapted further by others. It's all part of the evolution of games. Our job is essentially, to tell you about the current DNA of games and how that can influence the types of decisions you might make on the audio side.

GAMEPLAY MECHANICS

Let's start by examining very simple game mechanics. Early games were 2D and featured one screen at a time. The earliest games like *Space Invaders* and *Pac-Man* essentially gave you exactly the same level, as it came to be called, but would make the game progressively more challenging as it did so. After a while gamers wanted more than just one screen, so game designers obliged. One prominent early example of this expansion in arcade games was scrolling. Scrolling is a way for the game to proceed without an obvious level change. Scrolling can also be one way (like left to right) or two way, or in some cases in every direction.

Defender (Williams, 1981) is a classic, fast-paced arcade game. *Limbo* (2010, Playdead Games) is a slower, eerie, puzzle based platform game. Both of these games use the side scrolling mechanic.

The next innovation is contrasting game levels. In these types of games, the player progresses in some way though the level, like a maze or obstacle course until they reach the goal at the end, and then the next level loads; or perhaps it's a character going from room to room searching for specific items.

We now might have a reason to change the music, as our character or player is potentially in a different emotional environment than before. As far as sounds are concerned, it might affect ambiences or sound effects as animations change from level to level.

Evolution of Games
Action Game

A broad and basic category of video games, the action genre, contains many sub-genres. Nearly all arcade games from the golden age of the arcade can be classified as action games, which are games that emphasize combat in gameplay and require accuracy and timing to avoid obstacles.

Maze-Chase Games

Pac-Man is the best-known maze-chase game, a game in which the player navigates the character through a maze to avoid enemies. It achieved mainstream popularity and produced the first game character popular in its own right. The follow-up, *Ms Pac-Man,* was released one year after Namco's original *Pac-Man* by the Bally/Midway Company, a famous pinball game maker who had distributed the original *Pac-Man* game in the US.

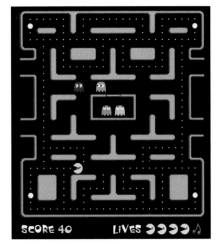

Ms. Pac-Man (Midway, 1982) was the successor to the wildly popular *Pac-Man* game by Namco.
Credit: Jeremy Engel.

Platform Games

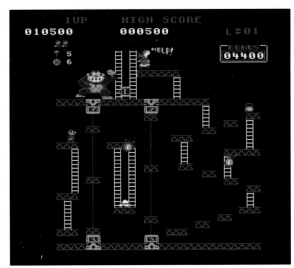

Donkey Kong (Nintendo, 1981) is a classic platform game.
Credit: Jeremy Engel.

In platform games, the player manipulates a character to jump or move from platform to platform to advance through gameplay. *Donkey Kong* (1981) is the classic example of a platform game.

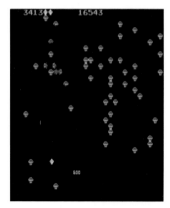

Centipede (1981) is a classic 'shoot 'em up' game.

Gauntlet (1987) is a well-known arcade hack-and-slash game that could accommodate up to four players at a time.

Shoot 'Em Ups

In a shoot 'em up, the player uses a gun or other projectile to kill nearly everyone or everything in sight. There are a couple of additional sub-genres:

Hack-and-slash games use only melée (non-projectile) weapons such as swords and axes.

Beat-'em-up games restrict gameplay to physical attacks with the hands and feet only. *Double Dragon* (1987) is a well-known early beat 'em up.

DoubleDragon (1987) is a 'beat 'em up' game.

Fighting Games

The significant difference between a fighting game and a beat-'em-up game is that a fighting game creates a one-on-one physical situation in which the player competes against another player or the computer. Fighting games may involve melée weapons or projectile weapons (but usually not guns). This genre includes boxing games as well.

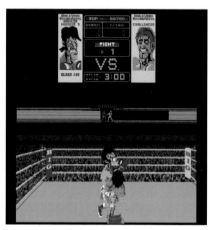

Punch Out!! from Nintendo in 1984, is a boxing variant of a fighting game. The player had a see-through avatar so that the opponent's moves could be seen more clearly.
Credit: Jeremy Engel.

Challenges

What are some of the unique challenges you might face when creating sounds for action-based arcade and console games?

Credit: Brian Schmidt.

Let's hear from composer Brian Schmidt. Brian's an industry veteran who's worked on tons of games such as *NARC*, and numerous pinball games.

“*Sound for arcade games presented some challenges not usually found in modern console games. Gameplay is generally short and level-based, and more often than not, a goal is to get the players' adrenaline pumping right away. So, long, slow, melodic build-ups weren't used; in goes the quarter, and immediately you hear music with a tempo faster than your heart rate. Although games were short, they'd often have a lot of different modes or mini-games within them, each requiring their own music. So even a simple pinball machine game would have a good 25–30 minutes of interactive original score.*

One of the more interesting challenges is designing sound that will be heard someplace with a lot of background noise. This means limiting your own dynamic range, since anything too quiet or subtle would more often than not get lost in the ambient noise of the arcade, bar or casino. That said, we would definitely hold back some dynamic range for the 'make everyone turn around' sound. That's a sound that signifies that the player did something significant—like defeated a final boss, earned a free game, or hit the really big jackpot. That would always be significantly louder and longer than any other sounds in the game.”

Shooter games, which appeared in the late 1970s, are three-dimensional offshoots of shoot 'em ups. Shooter games are referred to in terms of person: first person or third person. Although at first they were single player, later versions offered networked multiplayer gameplay, which allows a player to compete with other players on a local or global network.

In a **first-person shooter or FPS**, the perspective comes directly from the eyes of the character in the game, and the action appears in three dimensions. The only thing visible from the character is the weaponry they hold. This perspective provides an immersive game-playing experience. Although *Wolfenstein 3D* (1992) is considered the first true 3D first-person shooter, the acknowledged 'killer game' in this genre is id Software's *Doom* (1993). *Doom* featured all elements that have come to be associated with the first-person shooter. FPSs are now massively popular. *Unreal Tournament*, *Quake*, and *Halo* are among the most popular game franchises in this genre, and the *Call Of Duty* series is one of the best selling games of all time!

A **third-person shooter or TPS** is similar to a first-person shooter. The main difference is the perspective in a third-person shooter is from above and behind the body, vehicle, or spaceship the player manipulates. In this perspective, the character (or vehicle or spaceship) and his or her physical actions are visible on the screen. Thus the third-person shooter offers a more avatar-driven visual setup than the first-person shooter. The most influential early game in this genre was Eidos Interactive's *Tomb Raider* (1996). Later games such as *Assassin's Creed*, *Metal Gear Solid*, and *Resident Evil* have kept the popularity of the genre extremely high.

Unreal Tournament 3 (2003, Epic Games) is a prime example of a first-person shooter game.

Credit: Alexander Brandon.

Listen to what Alexander Brandon has to say about his music work on the popular First-Person Shooter Game *Unreal*.

❝ *In a First Person Shooter, whether you just want the core fun factor to be the main priority or not, it's all about immersion. Otherwise, don't bother. The player will be encountering things through the same eyes as the player character, so you want them to feel that experience first and foremost. Unreal is the most well-known game I've worked on and I think the score immerses the player more than the sound design. Which is rare. We did the game and nothing else has really come along like it. The audio design goes with the title, there were a lot of elements beyond sci fi that extended into fantasy genre techniques and the score reflected that, so the player experience was increased all the more in each location.*

A lot of what drove the player wasn't even so much their combat but looking around going 'wow, this looks amazing' and fortunately for us we got a lot of feedback saying it sounded amazing as well.

Also, I know this is going to sound terribly generic but each FPS is really unique to the themes that drive the game and how the player interacts with the world and makes choices. The Bioshock series even though they are considered a mashup of RPG and FPS, use a great deal of subtlety and dynamic range, whereas something like Halo 4 is a lot more based on steady combat rather than ramped tension. But its important to first figure out the highest priority that the design calls for. **99**

Music Rhythm and Audio Only Games

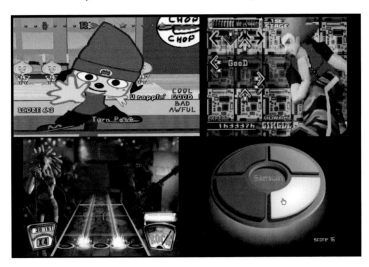

A variety of music and rhythm games. Clockwise from top left: *PaRappa the Rapper* (1996, Nana-OnSha/Sony); *Dance Dance Revolution* (1998, Konami); Milton Bradley's *Simon* (1978), co-designed by Ralph Baer; *Guitar Hero* (2005, Harmonix/Activision).

Music driven interactive games have been around since the seventies when Milton Bradley's *Simon* appeared on the scene. More recent games include *Parappa the Rapper*, *Dance Dance Revolution*, *Guitar Hero* and *Rock Band*. As the name would suggest, these games use music or rhythm as both a goal, and a way to dictate the gameplay mechanic.

59

Lately, there has been a movement afoot to develop audio only games. These games use sound as the chief design mechanic. The visual data in these games takes a significant backseat to the audio—almost a complete reversal of the way games are usually designed.

Adventure Games

Adventure games emphasize exploration, problem-solving skills, and communication rather than combat or lightning-quick reflexes. Adventure games usually focus on story and narrative context, so they share some features with novels and films.

The adventure genre started out using text-based interaction with the player, and by the 1980s had graduated to primitive graphics with the release of Sierra Online's *King's Quest* (1984), one of the most popular adventure games.

The prominent sub-genre for this genre are RPG or **Role-Playing Games**, in which the player takes on the role of an adventurer with a specific skill set or specialty (such as melée combat or magic) to explore the environment and progress through a storyline. All RPGs descend from the pen, paper, and dice game *Dungeons & Dragons*, created by Gary Gygax and Dave Arneson in 1974. Depending on the game design approach, the narrative, linear element of novels and films may also strongly influence RPGs. Another aspect of RPGs is the ability of characters to level up, or accumulate skills, abilities, and combat power, as the challenge level increases.

Combining Adventure or RPG with Action

The adventure-action game was a later offshoot of the original adventure game. As the speed and graphics capabilities of computers and game platforms improved, so did the complexity and quality of the game itself. The *Zelda* series is the most prominent example of a classic action adventure game. Current examples are series like *Fallout* and *Mass Effect*.

Action RPGs emphasize combat to the point that they often simplify or remove non-combat attributes and statistics and minimize the effects these non-combat elements have on the character's development. The most successful and best-selling action RPG is the *Final Fantasy* series, while other current examples of this genre are the *Elder Scrolls* series and *Diablo*. This genre continues to diversify and gain popularity.

Jim Hedges is a game industry veteran. His music has been heard in hundreds of titles; one such game is *Soul Reaver 2*, created for the Sony Playstation.

Credit: Jim Hedges.

" *For* Soul Reaver 2, *we had developed an adaptive music system that muted and unmuted music tracks based on the player's level of danger and combat. It was based on four game states: no enemies present; enemies present but not aware of the player; enemies aware of the player (thus running after them); and combat with enemies. As you moved up and down the chain, tracks would be muted and unmuted by variables based on these game states. The problem we encountered was that since the variables changed immediately from one state to another, the music tracks would be altered immediately as well, producing very unnatural transitions. I realized that we had to provide a way of smoothly crossfading between these transitions. I ended up creating a crossfade script that accounted for transitions between all possible game states which took me about two weeks to write and test.* **"**

Sports Games

Another huge category of games, sports games, are, you guessed it, games involving sports of any kind—bowling, wrestling, basketball, football, racing, snowboarding, etc. Whatever the sport, chances are pretty good that it's already been adapted to work on the interactive screen. Keep in mind, the very first arcade game with sound, *Pong*, was basically a sports title! The genre is largely derived from action games but the most popular and played in this genre generally have a realistic outlook. You already experienced two well-known sports titles inside the App, so you've got a pretty good idea already of what happens in these types of games. Here's a few more examples: *Pole Position*, *NBA 2K*, *WWE Raw*, and *Tiger Woods Golf*.

Sceencap from the demonstration video of the RUMR (Realtime User Music Remix) system in action in the *SSX* snowboarding game. The system applies DJ-like effects while doing tricks within the game itself.

Sometimes the audio team gets to stretch things out a bit. Ted Conley, the Audio Director for EA Canada, developed the RUMR (Realtime User Remix) System for the snowboarding game *SSX* that allows the user to dynamically remix any audio (including tracks of the player's choosing), DJ-style on the fly while playing the game itself. He created a system where various tricks, angles, flips, and player actions would result in different audio effects applied to the music soundtrack in varying amounts.

Sports games can come in all shapes and sizes. Clockwise from top left: *Madden NFL 13* (EA Sports, 2012); *Topspin 3* (2K Sports, 2008); *Tiger Woods PGA Tour* (EA Sports, 2006); *WWE RAW Wrestling* (THQ, 2002); Atari's *Pole Position*, MLB *The Show* (Sony Entertainment, 2013).

Going Massive—MUDs and MMORPGs

In the late 1970s, as text-based RPGs were being developed on university mainframes, the idea of multiple players playing the same game at the same time wasn't crazy. Eventually this setup developed into the 1978 game *MUD* (Multi-User Dungeon), a multiplayer version of the text-based game *Zork*. The coming of the Internet and the Web created the next generation of multi-user games, and although *Neverwinter Nights* was the first major example in 1991, it was Richard Garriott's (aka Lord British) massively multiplayer online role playing game *Ultima Online* in 1997 that cemented the genre as well as the acronym MMORPG.

MMORPGs resemble other RPGs, but literally tens of thousands of players can access the game at once. Though a player can play with or against friends, the player will encounter many other players in the game world. These games feature high-level interaction through chat or even audio (via Adobe Connect, for example).

The development of MUDs and MMORPGs led other genres of games to go the MMO route. *Quake III Arena* (1999) and *Unreal Tournament* (1999) are MMOFPS (massively multiplayer online first-person shooters). Blizzard's *StarCraft* series are MMO versions of real-time strategy (RTS) games. Recently, web-based BMOGs (browser-based multiplayer online games) have increasingly appeared.

Credit: Don Diekneite.

Don Diekneite is a video game composer, sound designer and voice director. His work can be heard in a wide variety of interactive titles from arcade games in the early nineties to the recently released *Rift*, a highly acclaimed large-scale MMO that went live in March 2011.

❝ *Audio design (music, sound effects, ambience, voice-over) in any game must account for two primary constraints: unpredictability and repetition. These constraints come into play to a greater or lesser degree depending on the game. Simple games like* Tetris *or* Angry Birds *for example have a certain amount of predictability in that you know what is going to happen, you just don't know when. In a large scale MMO like* Rift *however, knowing what events will happen and when they might happen is as unpredictable as it gets.*

Literally hundreds of players can be together in the same environment all with different weapons and abilities. They can all be triggering different sounds on themselves, each other, the environment, monsters, and/or NPCs all of which could be generating their own sounds as well. The environment itself is unpredictable. It may be night, day, raining, sunny, windy or still. It may be near an ocean, river, waterfall, in a forest, or a populated city. There may be dozens of NPCs, herds of monsters, or just one major boss creature all making sounds. The environment may include animated props such as windmills, machines, or vehicles. This list goes on and on. What this means audio-wise, is that no matter how well designed each individual sound is, or how many variations of that sound are generated in real time, it could easily result in a huge wall of white noise. On the other hand, it is also entirely possible that a player could be totally alone with all the sounds he generates completely isolated and exposed. The sonic world is utterly unpredictable. A lot of what we do is aimed at ways to mitigate this.

Add to these scenarios the fact that MMOs are never over. They are played for hundreds of hours, weeks, months, and even years. Repetition of the same sound or music can become not only tiresome but downright irritating (even if you liked it at first). So a lot of what we do is aimed at creating variety within a particular sound or music category. Perhaps the biggest challenge in all of this is the mix. Having a system that can respond to game situations and affect volume levels, priorities, ducking schemes, and the like in real time is crucial."

No Joke—PC Games Get Serious

Games developed on PCs offered a depth of gameplay not previously available on limited-memory platforms such as early second-generation consoles and arcade games. The new possibilities led to the development of deeper game types.

Strategy Games

Strategy games emphasize skillful thinking and planning rather than pure physical reflexes to achieve victory. Games in this category focus on combinations of strategic, tactical, logistical, and even economic challenges.

Types of Strategy Games

Although the genre of strategy games is broad and continually developing, there are significant distinctions among styles of gameplay. Leaving out board-based games such as chess, checkers, and backgammon, this genre offers two pairs of unique characteristics: real time or turn-based, and tactical or strategic.

Real Time or Turn-Based

Real time means just that: everything occurs in real time and happens at the same time. An arcade game is real time. Even if a game is an MMO, players usually compete simultaneously. Real time heightens the stress and intensity of the game as players try to complete goals faster than their opponents. **Turn-based** games take the approach of board or card games in that players take turns making moves, and only one player moves at a time. If competing against an AI player (or a very patient friend), a player could theoretically take as much time as he or she needed. This type of game usually focuses on a bigger overall picture and advanced planning.

Tactical or Strategic

In **tactical** games, the gameplay (or gameplay section) focuses on maneuvering a small number of units from the perspective of a lieutenant or leader. Tactical strategy games use small-scale plots and scenarios that generally do not require acquisition or maintenance of resources. The view is often three-dimensional and fluid. Especially in more recent games, the player can adjust the view to different perspectives.

A sampling of war-oriented tactical games. Clockwise from top left: *XCOM: Enemy Unknown* (2K Games, 2013); *Worms 3 Universal* (Team 17, 2013); *Great Little War Game* (Rubicon/Viacom, 2011); *Anomaly Warzone: Earth* (11-bit Software, 2011).

Real Time Tactical (RTT)

While there are many predecessors, the *Myth* series is a popular RTT title set in a fantasy realm, while the *Warhammer* series takes the genre into a mecha-inspired future.

Turn-Based Tactical (TBT)

This genre is not as popular as some others, but without a doubt the most popular series title in this genre is *X-COM* (Mythos/Microprose, 1994). In this series, the player reverses engineered alien technology and works within a set budget to command a squad repelling an alien invasion, on an isomorphic map. A recent reboot by 2K Games in 2012 called *XCOM* has kept the feel of the series fresh, and added a 3D look to gameplay. Another popular title is the *Blitzkrieg* (Nival Interactive, 2003) series, as well as a recent open source, community developed fantasy game *Battle For Wesnoth* (2005–present).

Strategic Games

Strategic games and strategic gameplay involve the big picture from the perspective of a general, an admiral, or another leader. Gameplay emphasizes planning and tactics at the highest level. The plots and scenarios are no less grandiose in scope: the goal may be to defeat Napoleon's army at Waterloo. The view is usually a top-down view of the entire world or region rather than of one small area. This world is rendered two dimensionally or axiomatically (in a three-quarter view). These games may also require less militaristic goals such as resource acquisition, food production, trade, diplomacy, culture development, and research.

Popular strategy games. Clockwise from top left: *Starcraft 2* (Blizzard, 2010); *Civilization V* (Firaxis/2K, 2011); *Command and Conquer 4* (Electronic Arts, 2010).

Real Time Strategy (RTS)

Although *Dune II* (Westwood Interactive, 1992) basically set the standard for real time strategy gameplay, it was their best-selling classic *Command & Conquer* (1995), that defined this genre. The game featured isometric views, a large map, and many combat opportunities, but it also required substantial resource acquisition and technology to maintain the player's military production capacity. Other popular titles include the *Age of Empires* series from Microsoft with a broad historical view, and *Starcraft* from Blizzard Interactive, set in a futuristic background.

Turn-Based Strategy (TBS)

Though *Risk* fits into the category of turn-based strategy games, Sid Meier's excellent, highly influential *Civilization* series became the gold standard of TBS. The player directs an entire civilization from the birth of the Stone Age to the future and possibly beyond by practicing the 4X rule: eXplore, eXpand, eXploit, and eXterminate. (Maybe they should have called it the 4E rule?) The player develops and builds technologies, cities, infrastructure, industry, production, and, of course, armies to conquer, ally with, and betray opponents, as the player sees fit. The player is the leader but must remember that every action has an equal and opposite reaction. The gameplay balance in *Civilization* became the model for turn-based strategy games of all types.

Credit: Kent Jolly.

Kent Jolly, Audio Director at Electronic/Arts has worked on the *SimCity* series since *SimCity 3000*, *The Sims*, *The Sims2*, and *Spore*. Here's his take on the special challenges involved in designing sound for strategy games:

" *There are several things about working on Strategy/Simulation games that I think are different from other genres. First, there's the fact that the camera view is usually a displaced 'God' type view. Accurate 3D sound sources often work against you when you want to highlight particular actions or areas of the screen. So, a continuous loud sound might be tuned just right for when you are looking right at it, but all wrong for when it's off center or off screen. We implement a lot of non-realistic sounds to change the focus of attention to what matters in the game.*

Another camera issue that we run into is dealing with extreme range. In games I have worked on, you could be one foot from a sound source to miles from it in the space of a second or two! Rendering believable and effective sound landscapes for that means a lot of work on the level of detail (LOD). This means that there may be different sound considerations depending on the camera's distance from an object in the gamespace.

We also often run into geometry or object placement that is not predetermined. We don't have a track or a level, but instead a world or map that can be changed/designed dynamically by the player. We need to analyze the scene to determine the positions of elements. One example might be shoreline or a forest that changes location as players add and remove these elements. The bottom line is that you have to try and anticipate many kinds of sounding object interactions and deal with them gracefully. **"**

Test your knowledge of **gameplay styles and genres** by going over to the App, in the Classroom area, and clicking on the Word Search book!

Serious Games

These games require more problem-solving skills and longer, deeper gameplay than the previously-mentioned games. These kinds of games are often geared toward real-world scenarios, such as solving political crises, or providing deeper understanding of today's issues.

Educational Games

In this broad genre, the game's focus is developed around learning outcomes targeted to specific audience groups. Players interact with objects and manipulate variables in order to achieve these outcomes, which are targeted toward specific educational goals such as reading retention, math, and science. The more specific the goal, the more effective these types of games generally tend to be.

Examples of this genre date back to the early 1980s, when the children's computer game *Lemonade Stand* was a big hit on the Apple II Plus. The player was put in charge of a lemonade stand and given the day's weather forecast. The player then decided how many ingredients to buy and observed resulting sales. Current educational games such as *Ko's Journey* are based strictly on required learning standards for math.

A few educational and simulation games. Clockwise from top left: *Puzzler Brain Games* (Maximum Games, 2013); *Scribblenauts* (5th Cell, 2009); *Sim City* (Maxis/EA, 2013); *Microsoft Flight Simulator X* (Microsoft Games, 2006).

Simulation Games

A simulation game attempts to re-create the experience of specific real-world tasks. A simulation game might take the form of an arcade game, as in a flight simulator program, or it may be expanded to a PC application that, for example, simulates civic modeling for larger structures such as cities.

Early arcade games in this genre tried to re-create the controls of the original or provide simple three-dimensional imaging (in the case of *Battlezone*, for example), but the appearance of 4X turn-based strategy games introduced a realistic management model missing in arcade games, console games, and even simple computer games.

Around 1990, Maxis began publishing its successful line of *Sim* games: *SimCity* (1989), *SimEarth* (1990), *SimAnt* (1991), *SimCity 2000* (1994), *SimTower* (1994), and the best- selling PC game in history, *The Sims*, published in early 2000.

Many other examples of simulation games exist. Simulation games at the PC level may be considered educational because players learn management, organization, and planning.

The Rise of Casual Games

The increase in use of PCs and mobile devices set off a new trend in casual gaming: limited-complexity games designed for brief or impromptu play sessions. These games began to attract industry attention. Many casual games, such as PopCap Games' *Bejeweled* (2001) and PlayFirst's *Diner Dash* (2003), were puzzle games. Others games offered a relaxed pace and open-ended play.

Once the Internet, and especially the Flash plug-in, became standard for PCs, websites began adding simple, casual games as extra features. Commercial sites such as Orbitz and Nickelodeon, for example, use Flash-based games to entertain their audiences.

Some popular casual games. Clockwise from top left: *Tetris* (PS3 version, 2011); *World Of Goo* (2D Boy, 2008); *Bejeweled* (PopCap, 2001); *Angry Birds* (Rovio, 2009).

Recently, social networking has driven an increase in casual games. Games such as Zynga's *Mafia Wars* (2009), *FarmVille* (2009), and *Cafe World* (2009) are tied into sites such as Facebook. Although the games themselves are free, players have the option to purchase in-game items.

Credit: Peter Drescher.

Peter Drescher is a sound designer and programmer and has a lot of experience working on games in the mobile space. Here is his take on what it takes to create great sound for all things small.

*I like to say that the **only** thing that matters is how it sounds on the device. You can create the Greatest Explosion Sound Ever™ for your game, but when played on a tiny underpowered cell phone speaker, it might sound like a mouse fart. You can write the coolest grooving music track with a fat bassline and a booming kick drum, but when played on an iPhone speaker, all you'll hear is the snare and the melody.*

One of my favorite Duke Ellington quotes is 'You've got to write for your players', and that's true whether you're composing for Johnny Hodges or the Vienna Symphonic Library. For mobile gaming, your player is a speaker the size of your thumbnail (if you've got small hands), and so you need to design your sounds from the beginning with this frequency limitation in mind. Mobile games are not console games. They're not $60, 40-hour, immersive experiences; they tend to be cheap little time-killers, played while waiting for something else to happen in your life. Console games are a major commitment of time and money; mobile games are light entertainment, designed to be thrown away after a few uses. Because of that, mobile game audio is maybe less important than for Xbox titles. Some of my colleagues may consider this blasphemy, but I believe it's true nonetheless. I usually phrase it as 'nobody plays the game with the screen turned off', but you see iPhone users running silent all the time.

However, this may be changing as tablets become more ubiquitous, and Beats-style studio headphones become more prevalent. As modern games target mobile platforms, the importance of sound increases. And in The Future, when social gaming is done via The Cloud, the ability to communicate with other players via voice network, and share audio streams, will bring that elusive 'immersive experience' out into the real world.

Conclusion

By now you should have a pretty good idea of some of the basic genres and gameplay types that exist out there. New ones are being created all the time so, think of each of these as potential ingredients in a recipe. Put in a little action, add some FPS with a Hack-and-Slash approach, and an RPG configuration with some puzzles and leveling up, and you might just find yourself working on a hit game! The audio design for each of these games will also be an individual, tailored approach to whatever recipe has been created. Note that we're not even including settings like horror, sci-fi, fantasy, etc., which will also influence your decision-making process. Knowing the conventions, rules and standards will allow you to break the mold when needed. Creative audio design is an important part of what makes a good game.

In our next level, we'll start looking at sound design for games, and discuss the basic roles that sound effects and ambiences play in game design.

The Interactive Quiz for this Level is available in the App. In the main Classroom, click on the Quiz book to test your knowledge!

Bleeps, Blops, Clicks, and Pops
Sound Design in Games

The History of Sound Design

Throughout recorded history, sound has been used in order to express emotions, feelings and moods within society in general, and the dramatic arts in particular. Although music was a more common form of expression, the craft of sound design had its beginnings in the use of sound to underscore dramatic actions in various forms of theater, such as Elizabethan plays and Japanese Kabuki. One example of this is a thin metal sheet shaken vigorously to evoke the sound of thunder. Over the years, increasingly complex and intricate props and machines have since been used to create a wide range of sounds both onstage and off.

From Italian composer Luigi Russolo's fantastical mechanical sound-making devices called **intonarumori** in 1913, to the rise in popularity of radio and real time sound effects to enhance the drama in live theatrical productions, the creative use of sound became an integral part of the mystique of the middle of the twentieth century.

Thomas Edison's original phonograph used wax cylinders and could both record and play back sound without the use of any electronics.
Credit: John Guano.

If you're curious and want to learn more about this phenomenon, and to experience it firsthand, just go to the application, click on the Videos area and choose **Animation Fascination!**

These sounds were originally made fresh and could not be stored by themselves, but as recording technology developed over the years, so did storage technology. Starting with the first wax cylinders and progressing to today's modern digital workstations, the sound of almost everything you can think of in the world has been captured, stored for playback, and made readily available for later use in a plethora of productions.

In the game design industry, the term *sound designer* may mean many things. The sound designer may only create sound effects, or may also integrate the audio into the final product. For the purposes of this book, we will explore the basic concepts that sound designers should be familiar with. In addition we'll also highlight important tips to keep in mind when you're given the task of designing audio for a game.

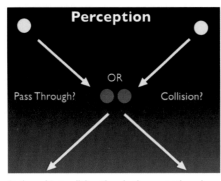

Do these objects collide with each other or pass through each other?

Sound fundamentally changes the way we perceive things. Games contain a lot of animations, and animated movement without sound can frequently be perceived differently than animation with sound.

In film, the creation of sound effects to correspond in real time with the action on the screen is called **Foley**, and the people who create these sounds are called foley artists. This branch of sound design is named after Jack Foley, who originated the art in 1927. He and his crew created effects for "talkies" (the first movies with sound) by recording sound effects (such as footsteps and closing doors) in real time as they watched projections of the movies. Their method required perfect timing so the audio synced with the action in the film. Today, although the art is still practiced, modern day non-linear audio editing from a DAW like Pro Tools means that the sound can be recorded first and then synchronized later with the action on the screen.

Vancouver Film School student recording old typewriter foley in sync with a video. Foley for games is recorded the same way, sometimes with and sometimes without the need to see the action on a screen.
Credit: Vancouver Film School.

In film and television, sound designers work in a linear way; they follow the timeline of the story, and the product of all these sound effects, ambiences, music and voice-over is carefully mixed all together. Once the mix is completed it always sounds the same when played back. In games, a cutscene, or a cinematic works exactly the same way.

In games, however, it's a bit of a different story, as we've mentioned. Because games are a non-linear medium, we can't mix all of our various sounds into a single file, because *we don't know when they might be needed*. As a result, we have to be prepared to trigger any sound at any time in the game.

When a game sound designer is working on interactive gameplay areas, all the elements—music, sound effects, and voice-over—are rendered out as individual files, and added into a database of code that calls the sounds when specific events take place in the game. In the game world, sound designers may create custom libraries by recording their own sounds or they may use pre-made sound libraries. In some cases, they may use processing and synthesizers to create brand new, never-before-heard noises.

In the end, the computer processor actually calls the audio on the fly in real time as the player moves through the world. In simple platforms such as most mobile and social games, the sounds must be pre-mixed (or balanced in terms of level) before they are triggered. In more sophisticated platforms such as console games, the audio engine can actually mix audio in response to the player's actions. These engines can act like virtual foley artists by adding signal processing effects to the sounds in real time. Note, however, that not all games are alike; the platform specifications define the parameters of what can and cannot be done with sounds inside a game—all of these can be different—which continually presents audio professionals in games with new challenges.

Let's discuss the function of sound both inside and outside of the game environment. For this we'll introduce a new term to keep in mind—**diegetic**. No, it's not a book by L. Ron Hubbard. The word comes from the Greek word *diegesis*, which means "recounted story", and refers in this case to whether a sound seems to come from the game environment, or not. Let's examine further:

Diegetic Sound

Diegetic sound is sound from sources that are visible on the screen or that are implied to be present because of actions occurring in the game.

Examples of diegetic sound can include the following:

- character voices
- sounds from objects on screen
- music from musical instruments shown in the game.

Diegetic sound is any sound originating from a source within the game's world. This can also be referred to as actual sound.

Non-Diegetic Sound

Non-diegetic sound, as you have likely guessed, is sound from sources that are neither visible on the screen, nor present in the action.

Examples of non-diegetic sounds include the following:

- the voice of a narrator
- a sound effect that is added for dramatic effect
- the music soundtrack.

Interactive audio provides a direct relationship to an action that produces identical or similar results. Adaptive audio takes into account one or more game factors (Health in this example) in addition to the action to create different results.

Non-diegetic sound comes from a source outside the game's story space. Non-diegetic sound is also called commentary sound, though it certainly includes much more than just commentaries.

- **Dynamic audio** is audio that is designed to change, either in response to the user, or in response to changes in the gameplay environment. Dynamic audio encompasses both of what we call interactive audio and adaptive audio.
- **Interactive audio** is a sound event that occurs in response to the player directly. In other words, if a player presses a button on a controller, the character on screen might move in

some way, and that event creates a particular sound—it might be a sword swish, or a footstep—it doesn't really matter. If the player presses the button again, the sound will re-occur. The sound involved is an example of a simple interactive sound effect.

- **Adaptive audio** occurs in the game environment in reaction to gameplay rather than to the user directly. Adaptive audio changes as the game changes.

Sound Effects Layers

You can further categorize sounds. Remember the big three categories we mentioned in Level 1: music, sound effects, and voice-over. You can break those down further. Since this level is about sound, let's look at the various subcategories here.

Background ambience is environmental audio. It creates the setting and mood in which the action will take place. These sounds usually last at least several seconds and may last a couple of minutes to avoid sounding repetitive. An example of diegetic background ambience might be the sound of water if the character were near water. A non-diegetic background ambience might be spooky noises in a haunted house.

Foreground sounds are the individual sounds that occur when a character moves around or encounters objects within the game space. Diegetic foreground sounds might include laser blasts or impact sounds when a character encounters an object. A non-diegetic foreground sound might be an announcement over a public address system to warn of an intruder, or a power-up associated with an object but not otherwise related to on-screen action.

Interface sounds are sounds that are directly attributable to the game interface and which the player uses to view status or change settings. Some interface sounds may be directly related to the player clicking or rolling over an icon or a button. Others might be notifications or changes in status; for example, there may be an interface sound associated with a player's health as a result of running out of energy.

Now that you know a little bit about what kinds of sounds you might find inside a game, let's put you in an interactive environment. Go to the App in the Holodeck Section and select the 'A Day In the Forest' demo. Enjoy a nice walk through a little mushroom village. A special place where you will have the opportunity to observe changes in your sonic reality in real time, and to experience how game sounds are triggered.

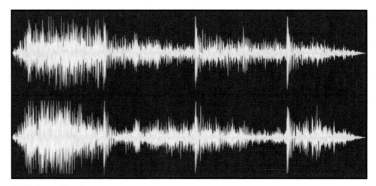

Credit: Jeremy Engel.

Formats for Sound Files

Sound files come in many formats. Some game platforms use proprietary formats, while others use open standards such as Ogg Vorbis. The list is long, so for the purposes of this course, we will look at a select few, the ones you're most likely to see.

Open, Uncompressed Audio File Formats

These file types are examples of linear pulse-code modulation (PCM) audio. The workings of PCM audio is a complex topic, but what you should know is that an uncompressed format generally offers you the best quality audio (depending on the sampling rate or bit depth the sound was originally recorded at). As we mentioned in Level 3, audio file size is dependent on sampling rate and bit depth. For example, a sound recorded with a bit depth of 16 bits at a sampling rate of 44.1KHz results in a file of approximately 10MB per minute of stereo sound or 5MB per minute of mono sound (also commonly known as the Red Book standard).

Interleaving

Besides bit depth and sample rate, there is another characteristic of audio files to be aware of, and this pertains to how a sound channel is treated in the file. If a file contains more than a single channel, it is referred to as an *interleaved* file. The term means essentially to join channels together. So a single stereo file that has two channels is called an interleaved file, whereas two separate Left and Right files with the same material are referred to as non-interleaved (sometimes referred to as multi-mono). Movie files can have interleaving too—in this case the video track is also considered a channel as well as the audio.

WAV is the standard audio file format used natively in Windows PCs for uncompressed (PCM) sound files.

AIFF is a standard audio file format used natively in Macintosh computers for uncompressed (PCM) sound files.

Open, Compressed Audio File Formats

Compressed formats take up less data space than uncompressed formats, but they lose audio quality in the compression process (how much they lose depends on the bit rate of the compression). These perceptually based formats take advantage of a limitation in human hearing called **auditory masking**. This means that a lot of data existing outside of our perceptual limit can be removed from the sound file, thus saving space.

The format of compressed files in general requires the presence of a **codec** (short for COmpression/ DECompression), a specialized piece of code that runs on software or hardware to decompress and playback the file. The encoder can process the files at a constant rate of speed (constant bit rate, known as CBR) or it can vary the rate depending on the complexity needed (variable bit rate, known as VBR). Be aware that some hardware devices and audio engines may not support playback of VBR encoded files.

MP3 (MPEG Layer 3) is currently the most popular format for downloading and storing music, and it is also used in games. 'MP3 files are compressed to roughly one-tenth the size of an equivalent PCM file.' MP3s can be compressed at a variety of bit and sample rates depending on the desired size and quality of the final audio.

Pro Tip

To make your life a little bit easier, as a general rule, if you know your developer is using a Mac give them. AIF files, if they are using a PC give them .WAV. If you are not sure, deliver both. This way you will mitigate the chances that the developer will have to come back to you for a re-delivery if for some reason software compatibility with these formats becomes an issue.

Pro Tip

One thing to know about MP3s is that they are not the most reliable at looping audio smoothly. This makes it tricky to use MP3 for things like ambiences or music. Using MP3 for triggering one shot sound effects or voice-over files is no problem, however. The reason for this is that MP3 was designed on an older, video frame-based approach. If a sound's length does not fill the frame completely, a gap is introduced that uses up the rest of the frame. This can cause significant headaches for sound designers and the solution is often determined by the game engine or platform that the developer is using, so make sure you ask questions and speak with the developer or integrator/ programmer about this specific annoying issue in advance of delivery.

Ogg is 'a free, open-source container format supporting a variety of codecs, the most popular of which is the audio codec Vorbis. Vorbis files are often compared to MP3 files in terms of quality.' Ogg files are not as commonly supported as MP3 files; there is no support for Ogg playback on any Apple device natively.

FLAC is a lossless compression codec. You can think of lossless compression as like zip but for audio. If you encode a PCM file to FLAC and then decode it again while playing, it will be a perfect copy of the original. (All the other codecs discussed here are lossy.)

Proprietary Audio File Formats

WMA (Windows Media Audio) is the format owned by Microsoft. It is Microsoft's closed source alternative to MP3.

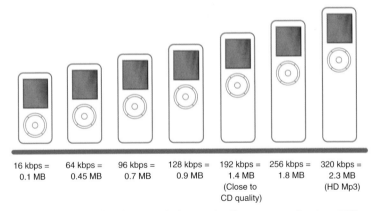

| 16 kbps = 0.1 MB | 64 kbps = 0.45 MB | 96 kbps = 0.7 MB | 128 kbps = 0.9 MB | 192 kbps = 1.4 MB (Close to CD quality) | 256 kbps = 1.8 MB | 320 kbps = 2.3 MB (HD Mp3) |

Chart showing a range of MP3 bit rates with relative quality. Measurements are based on a 10MB, 1 minute uncompressed stereo WAV file 16 Bit @ 44.1KHz

AAC (Advanced Audio Coding) is the 'format based on the MPEG4 audio standard owned by Dolby. A copy-protected version of this format has been developed by Apple for use in music downloaded from their iTunes Music Store.'

Other Formats

.AU is the standard audio file format used by Sun's version of Unix and Java.

.CAF Core Audio Format—also known as 'Cripes Another Format!' (respect to the late Jeff Essex). This format is the new

Apple-based format for audio files in Logic Pro and used prominently in iOS for seamless looping.

.BWF Broadcast Wave Format is a new version of WAV files supported by PCs and used in the Pro industry. They can be found with either .BWF or .WAV extensions. Pro Tools is now using BWF formatted .WAV files.

.SD2 is the once venerable, now obsolete Sound Designer 2 format from Digidesign (now AVID). It is now largely replaced with BWF WAVs in Pro Tools.

.MID is the extension for a MIDI file, which is not an audio file format at all. MIDI is a communication protocol for electronic instruments to speak with each other. It is non-proprietary and requires a sound-making source to produce sound. Such sound-making sources include external MIDI devices such as keyboards or drum machines or, more commonly, sound sets inside computers or platform devices.

Birth of Sound Design in a Game

OK, let's say you've somehow managed to get your first gig designing sounds for a game. Fantastic! But there's a lot of preparatory work you need to do before starting out in earnest.

Before you start any game project, you should know the scope of what is expected of you. Ask yourself and others the following questions:

What Kind of Game Is this?

Is it a side-scrolling kids' game with goofy cartoon graphics, or is it a big-budget console game with super life-like animations ?

What Is the Target Audience for this Game?

Is the game for adults, or is it for small children? Is the game aimed at boys or girls? Some sounds are more appropriate for certain audiences than others.

What Is the Pace of the Game?

Is the game fast or slow? Is it supposed to feel frenetic or mellow? These considerations affect sound choices. A puzzle game will likely have more

Credit: Raymond Bryson.

relaxed sounds, while a fast-paced action title will result in a more frenetic palette.

What Platform Is the Game being Developed for?

The platform determines how you will prepare the sound for final delivery. You can generally expect different workflows for different platforms. Also, the more you know about each system, the more optimized your sound design can be.

What Is the Audio Budget for the Game, and How Big can the Files be?

Sorry, this isn't what you're getting paid, but rather how much space you'll get in the game itself for your assets. It is important to know what you are up against before you get too far down any road. Nothing is worse than spending considerable time creating awesome sounds only to find out there is no room for them in the game.

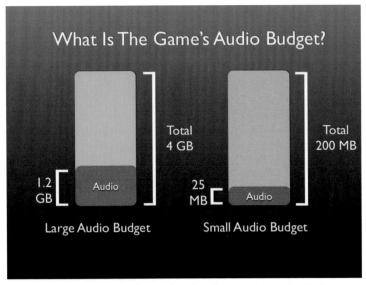

Diagram showing differences in hardware budgets. Sometimes you can be restricted by the space you're allowed, and other times you can be restricted by what the hardware itself will allow.

What Is the Hardware Space Budget of this Game?

Even if you have the financial budget to make all those cool sounds, you may not have the allotted physical memory space to put them in. This is especially true for portable and mobile games.

In many cases, the game designer or producer will have the answer to these questions. In other cases, you may need to speak with the programmer or integrator to get the information you need. Don't be afraid to ask questions—in game development, knowledge is king!

After you have gotten the information you need about the game type, environment, platform and budgets, it is time to start making some creative decisions. What will and won't be sonified in the game? What overall creative direction do you plan to take?

The Asset List

As you make these choices, you'll also need to create a list of every sound that will occur in the game. The document that contains this information is called the **audio assets list**.

This list is incredibly important because it is your master list of all the sounds that will be used in the game, and is also your road map to keep you on track during the development process. Sometimes the producers or developer will already have this information. Sometimes they will have it included in a game design document. Or they may have nothing at all. It's up to you to ask about this list and if they don't have one yet, go about creating it. Additionally, some companies may already use elaborate asset management systems to track each sound in the game.

Each item in an audio assets list should contain at least the following information:

- the name of the sound broken out by type (music, sound effect, or voice-over);
- a file name that follows a standardized file naming convention;
- a description of the function of the sound (e.g., car sounds or dialogue);
- an indication of whether the sound is looping or a one-shot (play once) trigger.

Pro Tip

We can't stress enough the importance of a well-thought-out asset list and file naming convention in game audio design. Without it, hundreds or thousands of assets (or more) will have no version control or description as to their function within the game. Imagine editing hundreds of nifty sound effects and calling them all SFX_01, SFX_02 and on and on. This is easy and quick to do, but when this gets over to the programmer or integrator who's tasked with putting these sounds into the game, without an asset list, they will have no idea how these sounds function or when they are to be called. In some cases, they'll have no way to move forward, and in others, they will have to listen to every one of them and try and figure out their function and rename them, and they will *not* be happy. So, getting together with the producer and programmer ahead of time, and settling on a coherent file naming convention and asset tracking system in advance is a very smart thing to do!

Example of an Audio Assets List from the Game *Kinderbach*, produced by Zephyr Games

KinderBach - Audio Matrix				
Zephyr Games Inc.				
Location	Trigger	Description	File Name	Line
Title Screen				
	End of Music Start or Continue	Background Music Loop		
	Entrance	Background Music Start		
	Entrance from Game Start	VO	KinderBack_Line___01	Welcome to KinderBach!
	ALT	VO	KinderBack_Line___02	KinderBach!
	Idle Reminder	VO	KinderBack_Line___03	Let's learn about music!
	User Taps Upsell Button	SFX		
	User Taps on Games Button	SFX		
	User Taps on Lessons Button	SFX		
	User Taps on Store Button	SFX		
	User Returns from Sub-Menu	VO	KinderBack_Line___04	Welcome back!
Credits				
	Continued from Title	Background Music Loop		
	Entrance from Title	VO	KinderBack_Line___05	These people made this game!
	User Taps on Back Button	SFX		
Upsell Screen				
	Continued from Title	Background Music Loop		

An example of a basic Sound Asset document, usually found in spreadsheet form. Get used to seeing a lot of these! For really large game they may even use a database to organize sounds. *Credit:* Zephyr Games.

In this example, the filename of the asset is listed in the fourth column. You can organize your list by whatever criteria you want. In this case, the creators of this game thought game location was the most important category, followed by the trigger of the sound (a button, an object in game, and so forth), the description (or category) of the sound, the file name, and, finally, a comment, which acts more like a description here.

Where do Sounds Come From?

Sounds come from many sources, some natural and some not so natural. The sources of sounds depend on the needs and requirements of the game.

Once upon a time, the only way to get sound for production was to create it yourself. If you needed the sound of a gentle stream flowing through a meadow, you went out to find a stream and record it. If you needed footsteps for a video, you created them yourself. For a science fiction feature, you might create the sound from scratch with a synthesizer. Shortly after the CD attained significant popularity, film companies and engineers began creating vast libraries of sound effects and making these libraries available to other designers for purchase. The practice continues today, but the Internet has changed the dynamics.

Industry-Standard Sound-Effects Libraries

Today, the open market offers libraries of all kinds, from cartoon sounds to ambient backgrounds. Sound designers mix, edit, and recombine sounds from these libraries to produce original creations. It is generally advisable to create your own sounds, but original sounds take time and can be costly. There is no shame in using sound libraries, but it is preferable to customize anything you source to avoid sounding too generic.

Sound Ideas and Hollywood Edge are two very well-known and respected sound effect collection makers, and were among the first to offer complete libraries of sound effects on CD for film and television purposes. They are still used frequently today, though experienced sound designers will often process these sounds, due to their overly common usage in the industry.

Downloadable Sound-Effects Libraries

With the advent of the Web, many companies have begun providing sound libraries online. Such libraries offer immediate access: the ability to listen to clips and download them on the spot.

A few paid websites with sound effects. Left to right: thegamecreators.com, sounddogs.com and soundranger.com. These sites contract with a number of established as well as independent sound designers to provide a wide variety of sound effects that can be purchased digitally and downloaded.

These websites offer free sound effects for designers on a budget, which can be useful, but are often of dubious quality and may require processing to be effective.

Free Sound-Effects Libraries

The growing open source movement means that often you can find sounds at no cost at all. But you must be careful to ensure that you have the rights to use these sounds in commercial products.

Once you have found your cool sounds, you'll want to insert them into a multi-track digital audio workstation (DAW) to edit and layer them. DAWs provide sound designers with toolboxes for recording, editing, and manipulating sounds in creative ways. Sound designers may use software plug-ins, and other editing techniques to create custom effects and evocative landscapes. The job of the sound designer is to manipulate sounds to enhance the events on the screen. Simple games may call for just a few sounds, while more complex games may require thousands. Let's go over some of the types of techniques and processing sound designers regularly use.

EDITING TECHNIQUES
One Shots and Looping

A One Shot file is a file that plays only one time when it is triggered. These were originally triggered from tape cartridges and used a lot in radio stations to create canned laughter and on the spot pre-recorded sound effects. The term has since developed but it still refers to a file that plays in entirety one time only, with no interruptions. A One Shot file should be carefully edited so that it starts and ends smoothly, with no clicks or pops.

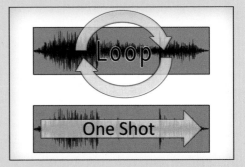

Credit: Jeremy Engel.

Looping is, of course, absolutely important, both from a resource perspective as well as a gameplay perspective. The creation of seamless loops in games is essential, because games are often indeterminate with regards to time, and you don't have a lot of audio budget with which to store files on the platform.

Loops can be of background ambient material, or of foreground local sound effects. Testing your loops for clicks and pops is a must. One common way to avoid this nasty issue is to make sure your audio waveform comes very close to the exact middle of the waveform on both the beginning and at the end—what's often referred to as a *zero crossing*. Other techniques of looping can include copying and reversing the sound, crossfading the ending material into the beginning, and many more.

Take it from us—learning how to seamlessly loop audio will be an absolutely required skill. Anyone who provides loops that have pauses, clicks, or pops, will soon find themselves having to redo their work. And unfortunately, even with all this sophisticated technology, you'll find that you'll be encountering this situation and having to deal with it more often than you might think . . .

Beyond the simple editing tasks that we've discussed here, processing audio with plug-ins is also a huge part of a sound designer's job. Again the categories of processing are absolutely vast, so here's our top 4 or 5 effects you'll be encountering.

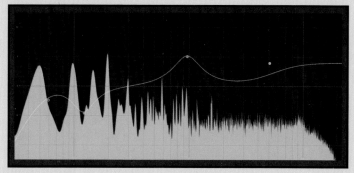

Equalization, or EQ, controls the filtering of the frequency spectrum or harmonics of a sound in order to produce desired results. This is very commonly used when preparing any kind of audio assets for film or TV or recordings, in live sound mixing and of course, in games.
Credit: Jeremy Engel.

Equalization

Filtering or equalization (EQ for short) affects the entire frequency spectrum of a sound. You already know that you can hear from 20Hz to 20KHz in the prime of your life. But you may not be aware that every note from an instrument or any sound you hear actually contains a complex array of frequencies or pitches occurring simultaneously. Each of these individual frequencies is called a **harmonic**; the combination of all harmonics in a particular relationship creates the sonic differences between a human voice, a guitar, an explosion, and the squeal of brakes. Each of these sounds has a definable frequency range, starting with the fundamental (the lowest harmonic—there may be more than one of these in more noise-like sounds) and proceeding up through what is called a harmonic series. Harmonics are often perceived in terms of the color and the quality of the sound.

Diagram of Compression/Limiting: When a signal passes over a particular threshold level, its dynamic range is reduced. This signal can then be increased in overall volume afterwards, resulting in a much louder sound. Compression will still allow the input signal to increase in level, while limiting will keep the sound held to the level of the threshold regardless of input volume. Compression/Limiting is an extremely common effect to use both in asset preparation and mixing/mastering.
Credit: Jeremy Engel and Scott Looney.

In general, the more harmonics a sound has, the brighter and buzzier the sound will be. Higher harmonics add a buzzy, thin quality to a sound; lower harmonics add roundness and fullness. Reducing the number of higher harmonics makes the sound rounder, duller, and more muffled. Starting from the fundamental and eliminating lower frequencies makes the sound thinner and buzzier; the sound loses its body. All sounds have a wide frequency spectrum; changing or emphasizing areas of EQ can make a phone call sound as though it is coming through a small speaker or a call from headquarters sound as though it is being played inside a helmet, like in *Halo*. EQ also plays a vital role in the final mix of a game; the proper use of EQ puts all sounds in the proper places, so they can be clearly delineated in the final mix.

Compression

Unlike the compression discussed earlier, this type of compression does not reduce file size; instead, it reduces dynamic range. This compression is accomplished through automatic detection of a certain threshold. If an audio signal goes over this threshold, the output level is reduced in volume. That may not sound useful, but if the reduced audio is then increased in volume, the result is a much louder and more present sound. In a game, compression can be very useful in balancing out the volume levels of a multitude of different audio files and channels.

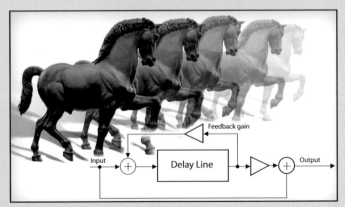

Diagram of Delay effect: Although based on a simple concept similar to an echo, the effect is then 'fed back' to the input to produce repeated echoes, eventually fading out to silence, as shown here with the horse sculptures.
Credit: Jeremy Engel.

Delay

Delay is a popular form of time manipulation, closely related to echo. Delay can be used to create a variety of effects. Multiple delays (often called tap delays) can make a character sound as though he is on the surface of the moon or make a single pair of horse hooves sound like a pack of wild ponies.

Reverberation

Another common effect is reverb (short for reverberation) to simulate various environments. Reverberation results from a sound bouncing off every available surface in an enclosed space. Imagine the acoustics in a large church or a big concert hall. Now imagine what footsteps would sound like in a place that large. Reverb is a dynamic effect that changes when a character enters a new room of a different size.

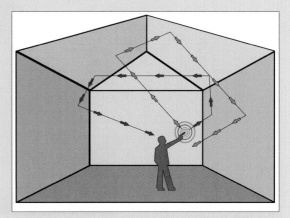

Diagram of Reverb effect: If the man in the picture was shooting a blank instead of a bullet, the sound from the gun would reflect off every surface in an enclosed area until its energy was used up. These reflections then get summed up together as reverb.

Sound Layering

One of the most common sound-design techniques is layering, which involves creating a new sound from a combination of sounds. For example, the sound of a bat hitting a baseball may consist of four sounds mixed together. The first layer may be a live recording of a baseball player hitting a ball with a simple wood bat. The second layer may add an extra-low end by combining the impact thud of a pile driver as it pounds a large stake into the earth. The third layer may introduce the explosion of a firing gun, and the fourth layer may add the sound of a large piece of paper catching on fire. When all four elements are mixed together, the resulting sound becomes the perfect accompaniment to an animation of a batter hitting a ball so hard that it bursts into flames in the game.

3D Sound

3D sound has become very popular in games. It is common to have a sound enter from one side of the screen and exit on the other. Other sounds play differently as they move front to back on screen. Special recording techniques called binaural recording are used to create three-dimensional sound fields that appear larger than life when listened to through headphones. Still other systems use surround-sound speaker placement to produce the effect of sounds coming from the side of or behind a player. These techniques enhance the player's immersion in the artificial environment and create a sense of realism or, in some cases, hyper-realism. In most cases, spatial sound is accomplished in the game engine or in audio middleware. You don't have to worry about 3D sound within a DAW, but you do have to prepare the sound for triggering within the game engine.

A sound designer at work, editing foley.
Credit: Vancouver Film School.

Creating Your Own Sounds

When designing your own sound effects, you should always keep an open mind. Let your imagination, eyes, and ears provide the answer. There is no one right or wrong way to design sound; this is a creative process with many solutions. In some cases, you may need very realistic sounds; in others cases, synthesized sounds may work better. You must consider every sound in relation to visual action. Sounds heard by themselves, while technically accurate, may not come across right when they are married to images and animations on screen. It is a strange phenomenon, but one you will find to be true.

It's always a good idea to record and edit your own custom sounds. Creating a custom library is a huge subject and a complex endeavor. In this book we are going to concentrate a bit more on the editing part rather than the recording. We do provide a few recording tips and tricks on page 115, in Level 7 of this book. All of the information below should also apply quite well to any custom library's.

Let's go over some advice for you to consider as you are sourcing and editing sound effects.

Use Synonyms

When you are searching for sounds, think of synonyms. For example, if you want a creaking sound, you might also search for the word 'stretching.'

Go General

If you can't find something in a specific search, sometimes searching for general categories helps. Let's say you are looking for the sound of a horse galloping. Instead of searching for 'horse galloping,' search for the term 'horse' to see how many matches and variations turn up.

Listen to the Whole Sound

You may find a sound buried within the audio of another sound. For example, let's say you need to provide a hoof clop. If you are having no luck finding anything useful, you might generalize your search and find a minute-long ambient recording of a horse cart passing in front of somebody in Italy. This file might contain a couple of isolated horse clops that are perfect for your project. You can cut these sounds out of the original file to obtain the sounds you need.

Think Interesting and Original

When you are using existing sound effects, find interesting and original ways to edit or process sounds. Many sounds are well defined in the genre and regarded as instant clichés when they are heard.

A perfect example of such a recognizable sound is the Wilhelm Scream. This sound, which originated in the 1950s, has been around the block numerous times, yet it's still a good sound due to its over-the-top

This screencap from the movie *Distant Drums* shows the first recorded use of the Wilhelm Scream (originally titled 'Man Being Eaten by an Alligator'), which predated the *Charge At Feather River* movie scene that has since become synonymous with the Wilhelm character. From the movie *Jungle Drums*.

intensity. Its original title was 'Man Getting Eaten by Alligator', and it originally came from the 1951 movie *Distant Drums*. However, the name 'Wilhelm' came from a character in a later film from 1953 called *Charge At Feather River*, which used the same sound for a scene where he gets struck by an arrow in the leg. You can thank Ben Burtt, the sound designer of the *Star Wars* films, for the revived popularity of the Wilhelm Scream. The Wilhelm Scream is used in every *Star Wars* movie— sometimes more than once!

In all cases, spend time polishing your sounds and making them as creative and original as possible. Elegant design takes time and is well worth the effort. You will also want to spend time fitting your sounds into the smallest footprint possible. Tight editing and file size conservation is always at the top of the list for game sound—file size matters!

Meet the Team

Over the years, the team of sound designers dedicated to game projects has grown. The following is a short list of the different jobs performed by sound designers on a range of games, from mobile games to AAA titles. Keep in mind that in smaller companies, many of these jobs are done by the same person. For the purposes of this level, we are breaking them out into the most general categories that you are likely to find out in the field.

Audio Director

The audio director oversees teams of audio designers, and usually directs those teams as they work on multiple titles simultaneously. The audio director will deal with everything from resources and schedules, to hiring talent. Most importantly, the audio director works with the game designer and producers to develop a coherent overall vision and sonic concept for the game, then translates that vision to the audio leads and designers who will bring it to life inside the game.

Audio Lead

The audio lead coordinates all the audio for a single game title. In smaller companies, where there is not as much simultaneous game development, the audio director and audio lead may in fact be the same person. It is not uncommon for an audio lead to create game assets, as well as meet with the game designers and producers on a regular basis during the production cycle.

Sound Designer

The sound designer creates sounds of all types for games using digital audio workstations and other sound-editing programs to blend natural and electronic sounds. As discussed, these sounds may be custom made using foley techniques, synthesis, or sourced from sound-effect libraries. In some cases, the sound designer may also find themselves implementing the audio they create into the game they are working on using a variety of tools. These tools may be off-the-shelf popular middleware applications or proprietary software developed by in-house programmers.

Audio Programmer

The integrator, or programmer, works with a game engine, middleware, and other production tools to integrate all sounds into the game. Programmers are not usually given the role of designing sounds. They have coding experience with languages like C++, Objective-C, Python and more, to go along with a deep knowledge of audio systems and hardware capabilities. Audio programmers often write custom applications and tools that are used by the rest of the creative team.

Conclusion

So as you can see, there's a lot of things to keep in mind when designing sounds for games. On the one hand the process of creating or sourcing the sound is nearly identical to what you'd do when making sounds for film or TV, but on the other hand, the open-ended nature of sounds in a gaming environment means the sound has to potentially react dynamically at each moment. Sounds can be directly linked to player actions, or to open-ended looping backgrounds. In addition, we see that keeping track of exactly which sound has triggered is as integral to the game audio process as designing the sound itself. And if that wasn't enough, you have to contend with constantly changing software and hardware standards. A good game audio sound designer, is also somewhat of a technical evangelist, so it becomes part of your job to know what's possible and what's not. It's definitely a crazy mixed up world out there, being a game audio denizen.

The Interactive Quiz for this Level is available in the App. In the main Classroom, click on the Quiz book to test your knowledge!

Compose Yourself!
The Art of Composing for Games

Learning Outcomes:
Identify differences between linear and non-linear music composition ·
Examine the use of loops, branching, and transitions ·
Recognize the factors involved in non-linear scoring ·
Understand vertical and horizontal musical concepts ·

Music Creation for Media

Writing music for any kind of media is a form-follows-function situation. When left alone with nothing to look at and no deadlines to meet, a composer will, in most cases, write very different music from the music that same composer would write for theater, film or television. The challenges in writing for these mediums include understanding the aesthetic principles of the medium and working with the production team to produce a satisfying user experience. As you well know by now, the main difference in game music is that the experience is open-ended and thus possesses a very different set of challenges for the composer.

With a game score, you have no idea how long a player will remain in a certain location in the game. You also don't know what path that player will take to move through the game world. The challenge here is to make music that won't drive the player crazy by being too short and won't drive the producer crazy by being too long and thus taking up too much file space.

To solve these issues, a composer may create a piece of music that can be broken into many smaller pieces of music and work together as a whole, no matter what is going on in the game. It's a different aesthetic approach and an interesting compositional challenge to write music that can fit together like a puzzle in many different ways. Another thing to keep in mind is that games can be long—a film is usually about two hours long. Now imagine writing music for a game that is made to be played for as long as 100 hours! Yikes, that is potentially a lot of music!

Image adapted by Scott Looney from Sam Catanzaro.

Game composers face a host of issues and challenges that don't exist in linear mediums. The complexities and requirements of the game environment raise many questions:

- If you don't know how long the player will stay in a game level, how long should you make the piece of music for that level?
- If the action and intensity speed up as the player goes further into the level, should the music speed up and slow down as well?
- Will the music sound different on different devices?
- How do I know what format to deliver my music in?

A NEW BREED OF COMPOSER

Video games came of age during the 1970s with the release of titles such as *Pong* and *Space Invaders*. At the time, audio-recording technology had not yet entered the digital age. The standard platforms of the day—phonograph records and cassette tapes—were clunky, expensive, and hard or next-to-impossible to integrate into games. It is no wonder that game developers turned to digital music generation. Although the commercial music market would have nothing to do with it at the time, the use of synthesis to generate musical tones was state of the art in the game world. Games used specialized computer chips called tone generators that were programmed to generate primitive real-time synthesizer music that was then outputted to speakers. Thus was born a new breed of computer musician: one who used cutting-edge, low-budget technologies to create musical soundtracks. Ironically, these days, chip music is hugely popular, frequently performed live, and even arranged for full orchestras in sold-out concert halls.

Digital music was limited by the very hardware that created it. Tone-generating software used simple chips that, in many cases, did not offer sufficient bandwidth to allow composers to write melodies accompanied by chords. With limited code memory to work within, composers wrote music sparingly or only for specific parts of the game. Still, despite these limitations, many composing conventions developed back in the day, are still in use. Looping music and using music only at the beginnings and ends of levels, intros, outros, and stingers all remain fundamental aspects of game music.

In the 1980s, new tools transformed the landscape for composers; now scores could be written without programmers. Writing music using General MIDI and DownLoadable Sound banks (DLS) opened a new world of polyphonic writing that incorporated numerous styles and genres.

There remained many limitations, however. By far the biggest limitation from this period was the inability to use PCM (uncompressed audio) digital playback. As a result, music for games was stuck in synthesizer land. General MIDI soundtracks did not sound nearly as robust as live instruments. Also, playback sounded slightly different on competing devices. These differences drove many producers back in the day bonkers. They wanted things to sound the same everywhere, and they wanted the music in the game to sound real. It looked as though they would have to wait a little while longer.

Questions, questions. In this module, we will look at many of the ways that a game composer deals with these questions, discovers limitations, and writes and produces great game scores within those limitations.

Modern Day

Game-music composers have always had to be clever alchemists, comfortable with machines and computing, and good at creating musical illusions for producers and listeners alike. Good game composers are part musician, part technologist. In the 1990s and since, a slew of powerful innovations have made it possible for

Credit: Wonderlyne, Wikimedia.

musicians of all types to incorporate any sound they want into their soundtracks. Maybe most importantly, as mentioned earlier, these innovations have allowed composers in many situations, though not all, to remove themselves from the technological side of content creation.

In high-budget console games, for example, it is not unusual to find a team of five or more working on music for a title. The team structure has allowed the composer to specialize once again; the music producer and integrator or programmer help adapt the music for the game. The process of creating audio for games is similar to the process for television and film: the composer hands the music off to an orchestrator, then to a copyist, and finally to the players on the soundstage. In other words, sometimes it takes a village. For a smaller game, you may still find a production team of one, with all roles wrapped up in a single musician.

These days, a game composer can go from recording a heavy metal band one day to creating a fully synthesized orchestral score that includes no live instruments the next. Platforms are ever changing and being adapted and upgraded. Each change introduces new tools to master and new techniques to learn.

Speaking of Music

Even early on, some game developers were aware of the benefit of having music in games. Music helps create an emotional connection that makes for a satisfying experience; it is deeply missed when it is absent. Music can completely change the pace, mood, and feel of a game. Let's review some of what a good musical soundtrack can accomplish.

• Set the Mood and Overall Tone of a Game

From a catchy title theme to a spooky background, music helps set and maintain the player's emotional connection to the game.

• Identify Time and Place Within the Game

Music helps set the time and place of the game—whether that be medieval England or the cold void of space—as much as any costume piece or scenery.

• Identify Locations and Settings in a Game

Is your character on the beach or in the bustling streets at rush hour? Music helps players identify their surroundings.

• Identify Characters Within a Game

Like a music theme associated with a role in opera, specific musical passages associated with a character can subconsciously clue a player into what is happening in a game.

• Establish the Pace of Gameplay

Fast beats can elevate already heart-pounding action. The pace of gameplay is highly influenced by music.

• Increase a Player's Sense of Immersion in a Game

Music helps draw players into a game by providing an emotional underpinning to the whole experience; music creates emotion.

GAME MUSIC FORM AND STRUCTURE

Music in a game can appear in one or more of many forms.

Cinematic

Music accompanies various cinematics within a game—whether they are cutscenes, introductions, endings, or story transitions. These pieces of media are usually linear and help propel the storyline forward or signal the end of a game level.

Interactive Gameplay

From menu selection and instruction screens, game backgrounds and loops, to victory and defeat fanfares, music plays a huge part in the interactive nature of a game. This interaction may consist of the following methods.

Looping means going around and around, repeating the same material. If the music to be looped is too short, it might drive the player crazy, but if it's too long, it may take up more storage space than the developer allotted.

Branching is conditional music based on actions in the game. Different actions lead to different musical results. In other words, music can be triggered horizontally in pieces. If the character goes left, play music A; if the character goes right, play music B.

Stem mixes (or stems) are vertical re-orchestrations of a piece of music. Stems are created using multiple parts that can be muted on and off and re-combined in many different ways to increase musical variation. This can also be referred to as **layering**. Although this is a great way to get more mileage out of musical materials, it can end up being less interactive, as it has a limited amount of choices available. Also, timing between layers may not be the most responsive or as timed to gameplay events as one might prefer.

Transitions are used to move smoothly from one music cue to another. A disjointed score leads to a disjointed experience for the player; transitions help maintain the continuity and the flow of gameplay. Games now use a number of transition methods to maintain the player's immersion in the experience.

A **fade out** is a common musical transition in which one piece of music fades out and another may or may not begin afterward.

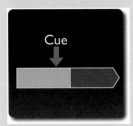

To cover a fade, a composer may use a special piece of music called a **stinger**. Stingers play over transitions to make the changes between pieces inaudible. For example, if you want to create a smooth transition from slow music to fast music in a snowboarding game when a character grabs a power-up that propels him or her downhill much faster, you might stop the slow piece of music at the same time that you trigger a stinger and then play or trigger a much faster piece of new music for the duration of the power-up. The stinger smoothes over the transition between the slower and faster music.

You can also **cross-fade** between two pieces of music, which is to say, fade one cue out as the other cue fades in. If done well, a cross-fade creates a seamless transition. If done in an abrupt or clunky manner, a cross-fade can create a jarring experience.

Cue-to-cue transitions trigger musical phrases end to end, so as one piece is ending, the next piece begins. The problem with this approach is that the composer never knows when the player will trigger a new segment of music and the transition may take place in the middle of a bar or musical phrase. Not the best sounding solution, as you can well imagine. Sophisticated middleware may feature quantized timing so the current sequence will wait until the next measure, or

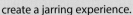

the next major downbeat before triggering the new cue. This timing can in many cases be controlled by the composer, expressed as beats and bars, or may require a programmer to translate the musical timings into something the game engine understands, such as milliseconds, samples, or frames.

For example, in the game *Shogo Mobile Armor Division* (Monolith, 1998) a system was created that contained a series of small files that enabled the game engine to analyze two cues and select an appropriate pre-composed transition. The cues used markers to indicate possible places in the score where transitions would take place. This meant that the composer had to map out and anticipate all possible interactions between different sequences—quite a job!

Music Gets Dynamic

Many developers, producers, and composers want game music to do more than just loop in the background; they want it to interact with the player's progress through the game. They want an immersive musical score that unfolds or adapts as the game progresses. The most famous example of early adaptive music is the music in *Space Invaders*. As the player destroys additional ships, the speed of the attacking ships increases, and the tempo of the music increases as well. This simple change created an innovative experience for the gamer, and established game music as a uniquely interactive art form.

Test your knowledge of **musical terms** by going over to the App, main classroom, and clicking on the Word Search book!

Interactive and adaptive music follows the same logic as interactive and adaptive audio, as we covered in our last Level. Some game scores are adaptive; some are not. Game music may be interactive in the sense that it triggers or plays at a certain time or for a specific reason. Think of it as though you are hitting a switch to make the music play when the player moves to a new level, for example. With interactive music, the music does not change as the game changes; every time you hit that switch, the same piece of music plays. Adaptive music, on the other hand, changes in relationship to the unfolding of the game. Each time that same switch is hit, the music may differ, depending on how many health points the character has. Or in a situation in which the player must choose the left path or the right path, the music may change key to match the mood of the new location. Current adaptive scores can tie themselves to almost any gameplay state you can think of, from player health to the number of times the player has been to a specific location.

Credit: Guy Whitmore.

Guy Whitmore is a game composer with more than just a passing interest in adaptive music. With stops at Microsoft and PopCap, he's spent a lot of time composing for all kinds of interactive environments.

Teasing Apart the Terms Interactive Music and Adaptive Music

" The differences between interactive music and adaptive music have more to do with the design of the game experience and the users' perception during the game, than with the techniques used to integrate the music. Interactive music occurs when a player is making game-play decisions based on what he/she consciously hears in the music, and thus is reacting directly to how the music is behaving. But with adaptive music, the interaction is between the player and other aspects of the game design such as visuals and game mechanics. The game-score in this case, follows and adapts to the state of the game overall and how it's being played, creating appropriate moods and gestures for each game-state while remaining largely subconscious to the player.

In theory, that definition seems fairly black-and-white, but in practice there's a spectrum that spans interactive and adaptive music, wherein most scores land somewhere between each extreme. A composer's intent may be anywhere along the adaptive–interactive spectrum, and a player's awareness and interaction may evolve over the course of a game. For instance, a player may become more conscious of a how an adaptive score functions over time, and begin using it interactively, to aid game-play or simply to 'mess with it'. Also, most interactive music 'rhythm games' very much rely on visual interaction as well as musical (to the extent that advanced players can play with the music off) thus making the score as much adaptive as it is interactive.

So the key for composers is to be aware of how their score will be consciously (or subconsciously) perceived by players, and to be intentional about their music design, i.e. asking the question: where along the adaptive–interactive spectrum will the score ideally sit, in order to best serve the overall game design? "

To see this how this type of adaptive music experience can work inside a game environment, check out the **Music Maze** example in the Holodeck area in the App.

Elements of Game Music

Composers can manipulate or change many elements to create different moods in a game.

Credit: Jeremy Engel.

Tempo

By speeding up or slowing down the music, the composer can achieve many different psychological effects. Slow tempos may sound ominous and foreboding; fast tempos may give the player extra energy. Tempo changes are often attached to the speed of the gameplay itself.

Key

The key is the scale or mode that an individual piece of music is in. Music in a minor key often has a sad feeling; music in a major key tends to sound happy. Take these characterizations as generalizations; there are many ways to manipulate keys to conjure different emotions. Some minor-key songs sound very happy.

Instrumentation/orchestration

The composer can change the emotion of a piece simply by changing the instruments that are playing. Trumpets make music sound noble and proud; bassoons not so much.

Go to the main classroom in the App, and click on the Videos screen and the **Audio Workflow-old school** example to watch and hear all about the first type of musical workflow in games!

Volume/dynamics

Volume or dynamics refers to how loud or soft a piece of music or a passage of music is. Something as simple as turning up the volume can make a huge difference.

By varying these elements, a deft composer can foreshadow events and alert the player both consciously and unconsciously to actions taking place within the game. Some video game composers get their hands dirty with the technology of the game platform; some have the luxury of using commercially available DAWs and delivering their music the same way they would any commercial production: by letting integrators take care of the back-end technology.

The Music Team

For the most part, and especially for larger titles, writing music for games is a team sport. Let's look at some of the players:

A **music director** oversees the creative direction of the music for a game. He or she meets with composers, game designers, programmers, and all other members of the production team to draft a creative vision for the music. The music director keeps everyone happy, so the music remains on schedule and on budget.

A **music producer** controls the creative vision of the musical recording itself. A music producer works with all the members of the team to hire the musicians and engineers and schedule the studios as needed. A good music producer puts all the pieces in place to make the final game score sound great.

A **composer** writes music, working in collaboration with the music director and producer to match the creative vision of the game. To create the score, the composer may use a computer-sequencing program such as Pro Tools or Logic or even, in some cases, pen and paper. Yes, you read that right: pen and paper!

An **orchestrator** takes the music from the composer and either makes MIDI orchestrations or prepares parts and scores so that live humans can play the music if need be. Orchestrators work with notation programs such as Finale and Sibelius to get the music ready for recording.

A **recording engineer** deals with the nuts and bolts of recording the music for a game. A recording engineer may record anything from live instruments to singers and needs a good working knowledge of recording studio technology and digital editing software.

A **mix engineer** takes the completed recordings from the studio and balances the instruments and parts to make sure the recorded elements sound great together in the game.

The **mastering engineer** produces and delivers the final tracks in the desired format for the game. Because this is the final stage of the process, a good mastering engineer has great ears and keen understanding of the platform the music will be integrated into.

Not all games have a large music team to produce the soundtrack. In many cases, one person takes on several roles. For smaller titles, you may still find people who do it all themselves: writing the music, recording it, and mixing the final product for delivery in the game. The number of people involved depends on budget and scope. As you can probably guess, the larger the budget and more expansive the scope of the game, the more specific the roles become.

Conclusion

As you have seen in this level, writing music for games can be both a simple and complex task. Depending on the type of game, and the hardware and software involved, you might be asked to create music in a very familiar way, or you might be asked to develop more complex interactive musical scenarios. The main thing to keep in mind is to remain flexible and work with the producer and implementer/ programmer to make sure that your music fits the requirements and flow of the game. This mix of compositional skills and technological know-how and understanding is what sets a game composer apart from a film and TV composer. How far down the rabbit hole you wish to go with audio middleware and implementation is a personal choice and there's really no right or wrong answer. There is room in the field for technical and non-technical composers alike. But in either case, a thorough understanding of the technical challenges involved is essential for composing music for games.

The Interactive Quiz for this Level is available in the App. In the main Classroom, click on the Quiz book to test your knowledge!

Do You Hear That Voice In My Head?

Voice-Over for Games

Learning Outcomes:
Understand the various roles of voice in games ·
Distinguish among the different types of voice-overs ·
Familiarize yourself with game voice-over workflow ·

VOICES

The human voice is a very powerful communication tool. Within a game environment, this communication is vital. Voice-over can do many things, from simply letting the player know what is happening at a given time to foreshadowing events to come. From simple instructions to major plot developments, the spoken word is a great device for immersing a player deeper into a game world. Well crafted vocal elements can produce many interesting effects, from the mundane to the sublime, such as:

- delivering important informational cues, such as basic operating instructions and game objectives;
- telling the game's story and developing the dynamic arc;
- allowing the player to communicate directly with the characters and vice versa;
- creating a more immersive experience and making the player feel as if they are actually part of the story.

It should be no surprise that voice in games is an important and growing part of game audio development. Games of all levels have started using fully developed scripts and professional voice actors on a regular basis. Games that still feature text bubbles seem out of date and old school. Some companies still try and go the route of not using voice-over, for the basic reason that it's time consuming and expensive. The costs begin with hiring writers to develop quality scripts, then move onto the casting and direction of voice-over actors, hiring recording studios, and the labor-intensive process of editing hundreds, or even thousands, of individual files. It takes a village to do voice-over work for even the simplest game. In the end, producing voice for games takes a team, time and meticulous planning.

In this level, we'll spend some time getting you familiar with the entire production cycle, from script to software. The idea is for you to get a complete snapshot of the process of how voices are used and produced in games.

Credit: Vancouver Film School.

Highlights in Game Voice-Over

Voice-overs in video games have come a long way since the Intellivision console introduced Intellivoice to games in the early 1980s. Intellivoice was based on voice synthesis—since the games of the day did not have much storage capacity, synthesis was a perfect solution, but it was a limited one at best.

In 1983, Disney released the iconic laserdisc arcade game *Dragon's Lair*, which featured some of the first human voices (as well as awesome hand drawn animation by Don Bluth). Due to a very limited budget, the voice-over was provided by the game's developers and animators rather than professional actors. Don't laugh, it still happens all the time!

Over time, storage increased, and so did the amount of dialogue. Voice-over became less of a novelty and more of an essential ingredient. A famous first of its kind example is the game *Seaman* for Sega Dreamcast (2002). *Seaman* included voice-over narration by famed actor Leonard Nimoy. Using famous actors to play well-known characters has become quite common in games today.

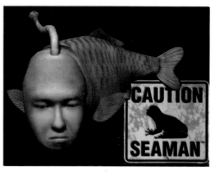

Credit: Seaman.

VOICE-OVER FUNCTIONS IN GAMES

There are a few different types of voice-over that are used in games. Keep in mind that these can appear in both diegetic and non-diegetic forms.

Game Feedback Voice-Over

These are character clips that tell you how you are doing in the game or give you vital feedback while you are involved in gameplay. It has become increasingly common for voice feedback to take the place of regular sound effects or in some cases be used in conjunction with them. Basically, instead of hearing a "loser" or "death" sound when you mess up, you hear a character voice say, "Oh no, that's not right, try again!" One common use of voice feedback is called "time out" instructions found in games of all types. For example, if a player sits too long on one screen in a game, you might hear a character voice give a hint and say something like "Keep going, don't stop now—click one of the giant mushrooms."

Narrative Voice-Over

Is often used to give instructions within a game, for example, before each level of gameplay. This can be either a long or short burst of dialogue that gives the player context as to the game's goals and objectives. You find them in games of all types from action adventure to kids' titles.

Dialogue-Based Voice-Over

This is by far the most common type of voice-over and is especially common in adventure games of all kinds. Games that feature involved plots will often have more involved dialogue. This most often occurs between two or more characters on the screen, but there are other instances, such as in sports games, where dialogue between offscreen commentators is used.

Who's Who in Voice-Over Production

As discussed, it takes a lot to produce convincing voice-over content for games. In fact, the list of factors involved is wide ranging and may even include places and objects, not just people. So with that, let's introduce our Cast Of Characters involved in voice-over production.

Producer

A good producer is a good person to know. Producers are the ones who have to make the project work. They must be detail oriented and good at dealing with people. Their job is to coordinate all the parties involved in the process. They will plan the meetings, set the schedule, deliver feedback, and make sure that everyone is on the same page as the production moves forward. Producers will also in some cases, help to write the scripts and oversee recording sessions. Whatever needs to be done, they will make happen. If they don't have the budget, or the resources to hire somebody else to do something, they'll do it themselves. It's the producer's reputation (as well as their posterior) that is on the line. When it comes to getting things right the first time, they have to be prepared, because nobody wants to re-schedule and re-record high powered voice talent—it's not easy—or cheap.

Writer

Creative writing is a growing and important market in the game world. After all, the writer is the person who imagines the lines that the actors will perform. They must be creative and practical at the same time. Voice-over just like any other media in games takes up space, so they must work with the game designers and producers to craft the appropriate characters and situations. Writing for video games is complex and very different from traditional media. A writer needs to be very well rounded and understanding of the challenges in interactive media.

Talent Agent

When the script is approved and ready to go, a talent agent is brought in to the process. They will contact the voice talent the producer has requested and negotiate the fee and contract terms for the specific person and project. Now, in the Internet age, it has become quite common for voice services to offer up talent online. There are a multiplicity of places that allow producers and designers to audition demo reels online and in some cases even hire the talent directly.

This is a quick and efficient way to cast for projects, as well as a way to discover unknown talent!

Services such as Voice123 and Voicebank can help aid the casting process when looking for artists to record voice-over.

Voice-Over Actor

Make no mistake about it, a good voice artist is a major talent, and like a virtuoso instrumentalist they use all the techniques they have learned over the years to pull off amazing performances under difficult and high pressure situations. Voice work for games is **not** easy to perform. Just think about this—the average console game possesses around 8,000 lines of dialogue. For a particularly long, epic RPG game, that number can even go beyond 70,000 lines of dialogue (that's not a typo)! As if recording all of that wasn't enough, there's more! Voice actors often have to record the same line in multiple inflections, so that the best take for the situation can be used in the game. They also have to keep the energy and pacing and tone of voice the same over long periods of time in the studio, sometimes days or even weeks—not an easy job by any stretch of the imagination.

Union vs Non-Union Talent

Some voice actors are non-union and some are union. What does this mean? Well, using non-union actors allows for a certain amount of flexibility in negotiating rates and availability. Union projects demand considerably more paperwork and come with many restrictions about numbers of characters, maximum consecutive hours the actor can work, and more, but there tends to be a higher degree of quality inherent, too. There are plenty of trade-offs. And ultimately, the choice may not be up to you but made by the producers or others who hold the purse strings.

Voice Director

A voice director works directly with the talent in the recording studio to make sure the script is professionally performed and well recorded. They will sometimes be in the same room with the talent and coach them on multiple line deliveries as well as making sure the energy of the reads are consistent from section to section. It is very common for young actors to use voice directors when working on children's titles. They help keep the kids focused on the job at hand, they are a friend in need and help to make sessions run more smoothly and efficiently. You can think of a voice director as a translator between the game producer and the voice talent. They speak both languages and can help both sides to understand each other. An untrained producer may not know why a line sounds wrong and may have a hard time explaining to the actor what they would like them to do. This is where the voice director comes in, because they know how to help a producer communicate with the performer to achieve a desired result.

Dialogue Production Basics
What Does a Script Look Like?

Creating well-rounded characters with appropriate dialogue is a must. The voice-overs need to be an integral part of the video game developing process, not just an afterthought. We also see that producing game voice-over is a different experience. So we again experience differences between movies and games. In this case, a voice actor for interactive media often isn't given a linear script. Instead, actors are frequently provided with page after page of isolated lines that are built to work together in the context of the game's interactive structure. The lines can often be listed as items on a spreadsheet.

Without understanding the narrative structure, voice actors will most likely be bewildered as to how to create a convincing, seamless character. In many cases a voice coach and producer will spend the time to provide the voice-over talent with a complete understanding of the characters they will be portraying, as well as the game's plot and interactivity.

So what does a game voice-over script look like? Scripts can come in all shapes and sizes.

VO SCRIPT/00100

Name/File	Take #	Lines / Notes
		[AUTOMATIC]
Hg_01.wav		Click to start the game
Hg_02.wav	/ / / ① /	Click to select your player
3 SAME		Click on me to turn me off. Bye Bye.
4		Rock on and have fun
5	Take 2 / ① / /	Mushrooms are for birds!
6		Birds also like Cheese
7	Take 2 / / / ①	Do you like Cheese?
8		Welcome to the music Maze
9	Take 1	Ready to play!
10	Take 2	Let's begin, shall we?
11	/ / / / / ①	Pecan pie is mighty tasty, click on it! — ALT,
12	Take 2	Chugga chugga chugga CHOO CHOO! All aboard
13	Take 1	Don't be so crazy, people will notice.
14	Take 3	They call me MR. SHowbiz

An example of a typical game voice-over script.

Recording engineer

While you are in the studio, you will be working with a recording engineer to get the voice-over recorded. They will run all the necessary hardware and software in the studio during the recording session. It is their job to make sure that the quality and sound of the voice is squeaky clean.

Tools of the Trade—The Microphone

As I'm sure you know, the studio engineer will use a microphone to record the talent. You may already be well aware of how microphones work, or you may be new to all this, but in either case, here is the essential information.

A **microphone** is a device that changes sound into an electrical signal. These signals are generally very low in terms of audio level by themselves, and require the presence of a microphone preamplifier to be recorded. Sometimes this **mic preamp**, as it is called, is built into the microphone itself. This is the case when using USB microphones. Other

RE-20 microphone.

Shure SM7 microphone.

times you might be using an interface to record that contains a mic preamp, or perhaps a mixer. Whatever you use, you usually need to boost the sound volume before sending it to the recording device.

There are many different brands of microphones and also different types. There are Ribbons, Carbon and Crystals (used especially in the older days of radio), but the two basic types we are concerned with these days are called **dynamic** and **condenser** microphones. Let's start with dynamic microphones:

Dynamic microphones are the most common for live music and pop music in general. They are generally the least expensive as well, and usually require no external power. Dynamic microphones do not evenly cover the entire frequency spectrum of sound. Because of this, they are usually used in specialized applications in a studio setting and have different strengths and weaknesses. There are a few well-known mics frequently used in radio that are occasionally used for voice-over work, but it's not as common to find them used in the studio.

Condenser microphones are more commonly used for professional voice recording, and are generally more expensive than dynamic microphones. They require external power to work, either in the form of a battery, or phantom power, which is a type of voltage run over standard microphone cables. Phantom power is more commonly used than batteries.

Condenser microphones usually have a much louder signal level than dynamic microphones. These microphones offer a much broader frequency response than dynamic microphones and are usually the tool of choice in the recording studio for handling voice-over work. Here's a few pics of well-known condenser mics:

Let's briefly look now at pickup patterns or polar patterns. These patterns are configurations that a microphone uses to detect sounds around it.

Neumann U87.

AKG 414.

RODE Podcaster USB microphone.

HOW MICROPHONES WORK

Cardioid, also called a **unidirectional** microphone pattern, is sensitive to sounds from only one direction. The pattern of a cardioid mic extends to the left and right about 180 degrees so if the sound source is directly behind the microphone it will not be detected very much at all. This pattern is desirable in voice-over work as it focuses on things that are directly in front of it, such as the actor's voice, and ignores other sounds that might be off mic in the room.

Omnidirectional This pattern is generally considered to be a perfect sphere. Unlike cardioid, this pattern can be considered the "purest" in terms of low coloration. It also responds much less to wind noise than directional mic patterns. This is not a great mic pattern to use in most cases, however, as it will pick up everything around it, including the acoustics of the room, which in most cases is NOT what you want.

STUDIO RECORDING SESSION OVERVIEW

Regardless of the microphone type used, the studio engineer will most likely be recording your session to some kind of digital medium and it will end up as a digital audio file. Pro Tools is a very common program used in studios for voice work, but there are other similar DAWs as well. Which one they are using may make a difference when it comes to delivering the raw audio files to an editor so it is always good to ask in advance what program they use for recording and coordinate with your editor so they know ahead of time if they can open the files the studio will send them.

As a general rule, most voice-over sessions are recorded at a bit rate of 16 or 24 bits and at a sample rate of either 48 or 44.1Kbps. Again to be safe, you should make sure to discuss this with the recording engineer beforehand, so you can know what they are doing and make sure that your editor will have no problem working on the files once they leave the studio.

Preparing the Space for Recording

To get the best recording quality for game voice-over, you want a clean and robust signal to start with, because it's very important—even more important than film or TV—to get a very clean recording that is free of extraneous background noise or any distortion. Remember, any noise that is introduced into the system from the start will tend to stay throughout the recording and editing process. Getting a good clean recording from the beginning is the best way to go. When voice-over files are compressed, noise can become louder and make the files sound bad to the ear. In some cases, if the voice-over is not recorded well enough you might have to re-record, which is definitely bad news and can cost a lot of money. Back in the day, when most audio was down-sampled and converted to 8-bit files, getting a

Test your knowledge of **all things voice** by going over to the App. Head on over to the Classroom, and click on the Word Search book!

decent sounding file was very hard. Today, the compression schemes are much better but a clean recording is still essential to making voice-over files sound good. In addition, you'll want to find a dry recording environment. This means some place where the sound does not echo all over the place. If you're really on a tight budget, and having to record the sound yourself, a great place is a carpeted room with lots of thick drapes, or a walk-in closet with a carpeted floor. Of course you'll likely have to stop recording or discard takes when trucks are passing by, or the neighbor fires up the lawnmower, or whenever outside sound intrudes. It's definitely not the best way, but the voice-over for the indie adventure smash hit game *Bastion* (2011, Supergiant Games) was recorded in an environment similar to this, using a skeleton voice-over crew.

However, in most cases, the best use of your time and money will be recording game voice-over in a studio environment, which will have a professionally treated and isolated space as well as a trained engineer. Let's look at how to choose a studio for your project.

Choosing a Studio

Recording studios come in all shapes and sizes, not to mention prices. Just keep in mind that a recording studio does not have to cost a ton of money to deliver good quality voice-over. Most important is the signal quality, isolation of the vocal booth and the kind of microphones they have available. Also, keep in mind that in many cases, producers and actors alike will be stuck in the studio for long hours, so the more comfortable the space the better. It's also good to have a place with plenty of food and drink handy for long days without many chances to take a break.

Recording studios can be found through standard advertising means, web searches and most importantly, word of mouth. Be sure to take a tour of the studio before you book your studio time—this is standard practice and studios are happy to show you around. This gives you a chance to see the space, meet the people and make sure the location and atmosphere is right for your needs.

In the studio, voice-over lines can be recorded in a couple of different ways. The least expensive method is to take the recorded lines of dialogue and have the animations sync to them after they have been recorded and processed. The other way is called **automated dialogue replacement (ADR)** or **dubbing**, also sometimes **looping**, used extensively in film and TV, where the actors have to look at the screen and time their performances to the animated character.

Editing Engineer

Voice-over editing takes time and patience. An editor's job is to take the raw voice-over session and cut it up line by line, creating unique files that follow a file naming convention set up by the producer. It cannot be stressed enough at this point how important a coherent and well thought out file naming convention is. Usually, the producer works with the programmer to define this convention, so when they get the files at the end of the day, they know exactly where each one is supposed to go in the game. Remember, in most games there are an incredible number of assets, each of which has to be kept meticulous track of. If there is no naming convention, things can get very messy, very quickly.

During the course of the recording session, either the producer or the voice director should have been listening to lines and picking takes. When they hear a line read they prefer, they mark their script. After all, if they do not choose lines they like, then the editor will be forced to choose the best take for themselves. This is probably not such a great idea, as they may or may not have any understanding or previous knowledge of the game. The other solution is to edit every single line, which can add drastically to the turnaround time and budget. The difference between editing one take per line and in some cases as many as ten is huge. At the end of this part of the process the editor usually has all the individual files on their hard drive as either .WAV or .AIF, high resolution audio.

The next thing the editor will do is to volume balance each file, so that when the characters are speaking in a game, one is not louder than the other. You've all heard games where this process was skipped, and one character is super loud, and the next super quiet. If the game is small enough, they will do this by hand, one by one, in a stereo editing program. If there are too many files (usually over a couple of hundred) they will batch process the files or automate the process in some way.

The final job is format conversion. Depending on what platform the game is being authored for, the final voice-over files will need to be delivered in a designated file format that works with that platform. For example, games with built-in Flash often use MP3 compression to keep the file size down.

To get an idea of what it's like to deal with editing and mastering voice-overs for video games, we were fortunate to get the expertise and experience of Jory Prum. He's done voice-over recording, editing, and mastering for well over 50 adventure game titles, including Telltale's best-selling and critically acclaimed *Walking Dead* series. Let's hear what it's like—straight from the horse's mouth.

Jory Prum has been recording and editing voice-over many years, and has recently worked on the *Walking Dead* series. Let's hear what he has to say about the process of working with voice in games.

Dialogue Production for Video Games

" Since the mid-1990s, it has become commonplace to have actors perform dialogue for all sorts of games. Some games make use of dialogue in limited fashion, such as occasional words of encouragement or simple tutorial information, while other titles rely heavily on performances in order to engage the player and plunge them into an immersive experience. If you have worked in video games for any length of time, you have probably noticed how much developers rely on spreadsheets as a method of organizing and managing projects. In fact, I cannot think of a time that a client has delivered scripts to me in any other form. As a general rule, though, it is advisable to migrate client-provided data into a structure that serves voice production more completely and allows better asset tracking and reporting. Developer's spreadsheets have a tendency to be continually updated and emailed around, making it difficult to ensure the latest versions are always in use. As a result, inaccuracies are quite common.

I have long advocated the use of databases in managing voice production, instead of spreadsheets. Databases provide tremendous advantages over spreadsheets, as they can be set up with reporting capabilities, are fully customizable, and can even allow advanced abilities such as incorporating audio playback of already-recorded dialog.

I mastered a project several years ago where the developer provided me with recorded and named voice files and a spreadsheet to reference the file set. I created a database record for each line of dialogue and added a checkbox for each of the five languages in that record. Next, I 'checked in' the dialogue in each language by ticking the checkbox if the file existed in the set I was provided. When I finished I could see that I was actually missing 20 percent of the dialogue, something the client was not aware of. The client thought they had provided me everything, as their reporting was crippled by the ever-changing 50-column spreadsheets they relied on. In my database I simply ran a custom report that listed each character, how many files there should be, and how many files actually existed per language, and emailed that report to the client so they could send me all the missing files and I could begin the job at hand.

In the studio, scripts are created from the database and then loaded onto iPads. Everyone in attendance has an iPad with a version of the script most suitable for them. We record one line at a time, with the writer providing context as necessary and the voice director ensuring the performance is consistent with the dialogue that will play before and after. Recording-wise, a single file is created for each line, making it easy to track lines directly back to files. I generally strive to keep the files as clean as possible, using a −60dB destructive gain change to obliterate any confusing waveforms and making life easier for the editor.

Next up is the mastering process. The goal is to ensure that all dialogue sounds good, is heard at the same perceived loudness and that conversations sound believable. Titles like **The Walking Dead: The Game** *are made up of usually a dozen or more environments the player will explore and interact within. By working on all files within an environment it ensures that there will not be a problem matching very large voice sets. When a character has more than 100 files, it is easy for there to be a bit of variance in loudness from the top of the list to the bottom, just because our ears are not 100 percent consistent. Mastering by environment tends to help eliminate this problem.* **"**

Programmer/Integrator

At last, the voice-over is recorded, edited, processed, named and delivered to the **programmer** or **integrator** whose job it is to insert each file into the game engine. How this is done depends on the platform. Most platforms have multiple ways in which audio gets triggered and it is the integrator's job to choose the best way for each game depending on the interactive structure of the project.

Translated and Localized Video Game Voice-Overs

Today, games are made in every developed nation on the planet and can employ talent across great distances. One of the challenges is that often a game is developed in one language and then "localized" to English or vice versa. For example, there could be a large amount of animation that has already been created and a need for actors to perform ADR. Voice-overs must be kept in mind when translating and localizing a video game for an international audience.

All too often, the visual aspects of a video game receive the most attention during the localization process. Saving the dialogue work and voice-over for last often results in poor translations and sub-par voice acting. A game that is visually stunning with an exciting plot is then marred by clichéd, confusing or implausible dialogue.

A good localization company won't put video game voice-over on the back burner. The success of the video game depends on every aspect of the game being the best it can possibly be. When it comes to dialogue, this includes not only accurate translations, but also the artistry and tone of the characters' lines.

Conclusion

Make no mistake about it, voice-over for games is a thriving and growing business. As we have seen in this chapter, a lot of people need to come together to do quality work. Game voice-over won't be successful if developers, designers, and publishers view it as a side note or something that needs to be added on at the last moment. Voice for games must be viewed as a separate world that is capable of invoking emotional reactions. Good acting and solid recording practices are a must. Quality voice-overs have become an absolute necessity in modern video games, and they are a vital link that helps the player to establish a solid connection within the world of the game.

The Interactive Quiz for this Level is available in the App. In the main Classroom, click on the Quiz book to test your knowledge!

Meet the Middleman
Understanding Audio Middleware

A typical game engine has an awful lot of things it has to do. In essence, it has to run an entire virtual world, complete with animations, shading and rendering, visual effects, and of course, a lot of audio as well. It must coordinate the overall interactive logic of a game. It needs to know both the location of all the rich media assets (including music, sound effects and voice-over files) as well as when (and when not) to call them. Even in a small game, this can add up to a large amount of data that needs to be coordinated. In a large game the scope can be most impressive, verging into tens or hundreds of thousands of assets. In all cases, game engines are software packages that make games possible, and it takes a talented and dedicated group of designers to program the engine to do all this work efficiently.

Now, in the case of audio, all game engines are not created equal— different game platforms have different audio capabilities. As we have seen over and over again, the history of games is a movement from simple to more complex systems, and audio system development in games is no exception to this phenomenon.

THE OLD SCHOOL

Back in the day, a sound designer made noises and delivered those noises to a programmer in some file format or another, and that programmer put them in the game in some way or another, and then they both (if they liked each other) went out and had lunch. Since this was a one-to-one relationship, it was usually a pretty efficient, not to mention tasty, system.

As games got more complex and people were not always close to each other, it became standard practice to make those noises and deliver them to a programmer, maybe over the Internet, along with a text document with file names and instructions about where these sounds were supposed to go and what they were supposed to do. This process is still in use today. But, over time, software has emerged that handles an increasingly larger amount of the heavy lifting between the game engine and the programmer, and sound designer. This software is called **middleware**.

Middleware Emerges

Audio middleware is another type of engine that works along with the core game engine and sits in a sense in between the sound designer and the programmer. Its main job is to allow the designer, who may not be a programmer, to have more control over how, when and where their sounds are triggered in a game.

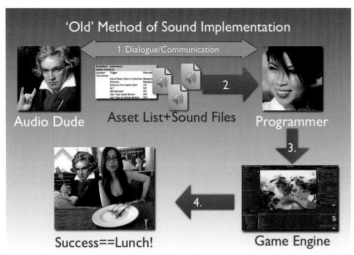

The 'old' method of audio implementation. 1: The audio designer communicates with the programmer; 2: The designer sends the asset list plus the sound files; 3: The programmer puts these into the game and configures everything to trigger and sound correctly; 4: Upon success, the two have lunch!
Credit: Images from Corinne Yu (Flickr).

Why Do We Need Middleware?

To see a good example of how audio middleware can be used, let's look at a car racing game. A car has a motor and when the car goes faster, the sound of the motor changes in different ways—RPMs increase, there's shifting of gears, and the engine sound changes its pitch and intensity accordingly. Using the old school method, a sound designer would deliver the appropriate sounds to a programmer as described above.

In this case, let's say the designer makes three sounds: car sound slow, car sound medium, and car sound fast. The programmer or integrator would take these three sounds and write lines of code that would trigger them, in real time, in the game as the car got faster. The programmer would need to take the time to program the sounds, adjust them and make sure they worked correctly during gameplay, and while they were doing that, they could not be doing other programming tasks.

Now let's take this same car sound and look at how it could be developed using audio middleware. First off, the biggest difference would be that this whole task can be accomplished by you, the mighty sound designer! Most audio middleware packages worth their salt provide what is called a **graphical user interface**, or GUI. So you would work in this interface, which kind of looks like Pro Tools or other DAW applications, and deliver a finished sound setup to the programmer. In this case, the audio designer and the programmer only have to know and agree on certain parameters, called **hooks**, that are used in the code.

Implementation using middleware. 1: The audio designer communicates with the programmer regarding which parameters or 'hooks' to have in the game; 2: The designer uses the asset list and sound files and configures everything in the middleware tool; 3: The designer/implementer sends the build file plus any bank files to the programmer; 4: The programmer puts these into the game and does not have to configure the sound to play—it just works! Yaaay! 5: Upon success, these two can have lunch or not. . . .
Credit: Images from Corinne Yu (Flickr).

Okay, let's get back to our three files, car fast, medium and slow. The sound designer will create these sounds just like before, except this time they will import them into the middleware program of choice. Once there, the designer will attach whatever is needed to the sound files. This might be crossfades or mapping parameters in the game to the audio. In this case it is quite common that the game engine will be keeping track of the speed of the car, probably in miles/km per hour, and the programmer will create a hook called **car_speed** inside their code and give this hook to the audio designer. As the car speeds up, this parameter value will increase.

Great! First, however, we need to create what is often referred to as an **event**. Remember when we referred to being concerned about the action itself rather than the time it takes place? This is an extension of that concept embraced by middleware. An event can be tied to anything in the game, and it can consist of multiple parameters driven by the game's logic as well. You can think of an event as a container for some kind of action or state in the game.

So now that we have the hook of car speed we can create a custom parameter in our middleware editor or GUI that is mapped to the different engine sounds we have. The value of the parameter will then control the timing and crossfades as well as the selection and balance of our low, medium, and high speed car engine sounds. It may even control the speed/pitch of the sounds—there's a lot of flexibility available here. It is then a relatively simple matter to export our sound files along with a text or configuration file, that gets delivered to the programmer. Now, all the programmer has to do is tie the value of the parameter to the game's event using lines of code, and voilà! The car's visual speed will now match its perceived audio intensity.

This is a very generalized example that should give you a decent overview of how the middleware process works. The details surrounding the building of complex audio events tied to game states and parameters can get quite involved. The main point to take away here, however, is that this is an all-round win-win situation. The sound designer has more control over their work, confident that what they deliver is actually what they will hear in the game, and the programmer doesn't have to spend as much time working on and worrying about the audio in the game. Plus theoretically, they have more time for lunch.

AUDIO MIDDLEWARE LETS YOU...

Define Audio Behaviors

Develop basic sound functions like when, where, and how loud a sound plays along with its behavior in the game. There are also lines of code that let you do cool things, like randomize sounds in the game environment (good for obtaining a more realistic or organic sound). It also allows you to prioritize sounds and create basic audio building blocks using reusable sounds, saving memory and time.

Create Dynamic Game-Driven Musical Scores

Middleware aids in the creation of sophisticated branching and looping structures so that music can be as interactive as the gameplay, or it can tie the music to differing game states, such as the health of the player. Non-linear music composition allows you to create music that responds dynamically to game events and musical transitions that may be as subtle as a key change or as dramatic as moving from one musical genre to another.

Mix and Master the Game Audio in Real Time

Many engines can connect to and mix your game live and provide mixers and snapshots, allowing the designer to tweak levels, effects, and properties for all game sounds while playing the game. These are virtual mixers that allow the audio design to change quickly, easily and efficiently (we hope) on the fly. This includes things like Reverb, EQ, delay effects, pitch shifting, normalization, dimensional panning and re-combination of sounds. This type of logic-based mixing allows the designer to create multiple libraries of sound that are chosen to play in the game based on a set of logical rules so the audio environment does not get stale with repeated listening as it is changing all the time in different ways.

Among other features, audio middleware allows you to create and configure real-time audio mixing in your game.
Credit: Laffy4K (Flickr).

Profile the Audio in Real Time

This allows developers to monitor levels, performance, and resource usage live. It provides a live visual representation of both the computer's processor and memory usage as the game is played, as well as displaying the signal routing within the sound engine—this is especially useful when debugging and optimizing your game audio. Profiling the audio performance of a game in real time is vitally important to making your audio system conform within specific limits, which is quite common on all platforms.

Create 3D Audio Environments

Supply 3D positions for the sound source and listener and automatically apply volume, filtering, surround panning and Doppler effect to mono, stereo and even multi-channel samples. Some packages even include an **HRTF** (head-related transfer function) mode to provide 3D realism through headphones. More on the specifics of 3D Audio later on.

Generate Sound Banks for Games

This feature allows the audio designer to create unique banks of sound that can be formatted in a number of different ways. The resulting file can take up much less space in the game, tax the processor less, and open up the use of modern day sampling technology. By developing high quality audio banks, designers can create hours of sound for a game, all within a relatively small footprint.

Deploy Sound for Multiple Platforms and Markets

At the touch of a button, most middleware can easily support a huge variety of desktop and mobile audio formats such as: Windows (32-bit and 64-bit) and Windows Mobile, Apple Macintosh and iOS, Linux (32-bit and 64-bit) and Android, Sony PS2, PS3, PS4 and PSP, Microsoft Xbox and Xbox 360, XBOX One, Nintendo Wii, Wii U and DS.

Compress Sounds in Various Ways

By supporting a multitude of audio-compression schemes such as: ADPCM, MP3, OGG, Opus, VAG (Sony's format for PS3 audio), and XMA (for Xbox), to name just a few, middleware provides a quick and easy way to export sound files to a variety of different gaming platforms.

Work With Various Game Engines

. . . such as CryENGINE, Unity, UDK/Unreal, BigWorld, Vision Engine and Scaleform, plus many many others.

It's really important to note here that a lot of this information is a moving target—implementation and functionality of audio middleware between game engines and even different versions of the same engine may vary greatly from platform to platform. When dealing with these various compatibility issues, research will be required to keep up on the latest developments.

3D Sound in Games

We mentioned just earlier that middleware can assist in helping to realize sound in three dimensions. 3D is now very commonly used and available in a variety of game engines today, and helps to submerge the player ever deeper into virtual worlds by adding more realism to game environments.

Various technologies are used to emulate sound behavior in this "real" world. Middleware audio engines help to provide the complex mathematical programming needed to simulate this real world phenomenon that we call hearing. Let's take a quick look and bring you up to speed on some basic concepts in creating 3D audio for games.

Positioning

Everyone perceives sounds differently. A sound card can emulate the position of a sound source with HRTF on two speakers or headphones. This function accurately models sound perception with two ears to determine positions of the source in space, also frequently referred to as a binaural configuration. Binaural microphones and recording setups usually use some kind of obstacle like a disc, or more commonly a sphere or a model of a head— or in some cases a person simply wears them like headphones. This is because our head and body are actually obstacles modifying the sounds we hear. This is an important fact—depending on where the sound is traveling from, it will reach one ear faster than the other, and this is generally how we perceive stereo in the real world.

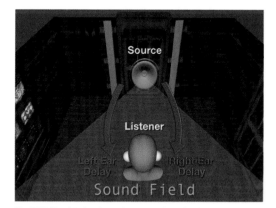

In a multi-speaker system, such as surround sound, (4.1, 5.1 or 7.1) the sound is distributed among speakers that are located around the listener's head. The sound coming from each speaker is positioned so that the listener can locate it. In principle, a normal panning setup is sufficient. This means there are several channels, depending on the number of speakers involved, which play simultaneously on all speakers but at different volume levels.

The HRTF (Head-Related Transfer Function) models the way we hear 3D sounds. The head in this case blocks out some sound waves coming from the other side. Each ear is like an independent omnidirectional microphone, and any sound will travel different distances within the space, creating different delay times for each ear. This results in more realistic 3D sound placement.

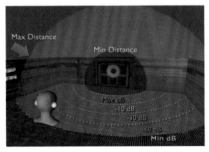

An example of volume and distance at work. The listener is actually outside the Max Distance radius—this means they will hear no sound. Going inward increases the sound's volume until the Min Distance is reached. At that point the sound will not get any louder.

Occlusion occurs when a source is completely cut off. In this example, the sound inside the room is heard cleanly and at full range. Outside of the wall however the sound is muffled, often losing its high frequency.

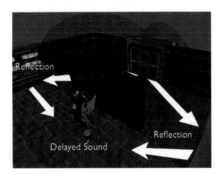

Obstruction happens when a sound source is not completely blocked. This results in the sound bouncing off various surfaces (rather than being directly perceived), which creates delays and/or reflections.

Volume and Distance

The farther the sound source, the quieter it is; the closer we get, the louder it becomes. Middleware allows us to set up simple models that raise and lower the volume level depending on the player's distance from an object. The sound designer must assign a certain minimal distance at which the sound starts fading out. While the signal is within this distance, it can only change its position; when it crosses a threshold or border, the volume will then be reduced by a curve of some type, similar to a filter slope but affecting the whole signal.

The sound will keep on getting quieter until it reaches the maximum distance, where it's too far to be heard. The farther the maximum distance, the longer the sound will be heard. In most cases the volume level is based on a logarithmic curve, because that's more natural to the way we hear sounds. However, this can be altered to fit the game's situation depending on the desires of the sound designer.

Occlusion

Sounds can be muffled by a wall or blocked by other objects. Occlusion occurs when a sound source is indistinctly perceived from an enclosed space. A perfect example of this would be if you were outside of a loud nightclub with the doors closed. As you get closer you hear more sound but the doors are still blocking the majority of the higher frequencies.

To simulate this environmental impact, audio middleware engines use filtering in real time based on a character's distance. When the character enters the room, the filtering is removed so that the complete source is then heard.

Obstruction

When the direct path to a sound is muffled but not enclosed, this is an example of obstruction. The sound source and the listener are in the same room, but an object blocks the direct path to the listener's ear. For example, open your door and take a listen to your TV or stereo while still standing outside the room. The sound bounces off the walls and other objects before it reaches your ear and as a result the sound is transformed. In a game, the audio engine can be set to account for varying reflection times, surfaces and distance using complex algorithms to accomplish this task.

Environment Morphing

You're probably already aware that the use of reverb in various types of game environments is very common. How different sound environments transition from one to another is a good example of environmental morphing. Your character can be walking from an outdoor environment into a church, or simply from one room to another. These transitions can morph smoothly or they can be sudden and dramatic. It all depends on the requirements of the game and design approach.

Audio Engine Needs

Basic audio functionality is fairly consistent from game to game. Audio designers at minimum want to be able to start a sound and stop a sound, loop a sound, change the pitch of a sound, or any number of other standard audio operations. Programming even this apparently simple functionality efficiently, however, can be a financial and technical challenge. If you are running a company that is in the process of building a game engine, you might not even want to try and add audio features to your engine. Instead, you might want to license some pre-existing audio technology that has a full feature set and is ready to plug and play. Nearly all middleware tools will try to provide a comprehensive set of features to cover these basic audio engine requirements, as well as the more complex ones we discussed earlier.

Here is a short, platform agnostic overview of what you will find in most audio middleware on the market today. Bear in mind that this is a very general look and the specifics can vary greatly.

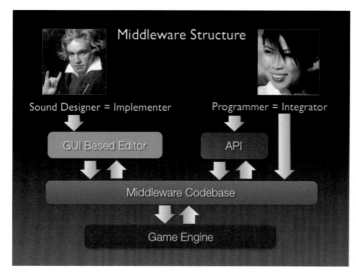

In this image we clearly see the split in functionality for middleware. Composers and sound designers use the GUI-based editor application, while programmers either work with the API or sometimes with the codebase. *Credit:* Images from Corinne Yu (Flickr).

Audio Middleware Structure

Most middleware out there consists of a programmed codebase that is split into two major sections or areas. The first and most important to us is the aforementioned GUI. This section, set up in a separate application usually, is primarily set up for the audio designer to import, configure and test their audio in. Its main purpose is to allow the non-code-savvy composer or sound designer to become a sound **implementer**. There are a lot of different ways that this can be accomplished, from making the interface look familiar, to creating completely unique views and configurations.

One fairly common look is a multi-track editor view. As mentioned previously, these environments look similar to a standard DAW but with extra layers of interactive tools. These graphic editors allow you to create complex layered sound structures, such as car engines, weapons, background ambiences, crowd simulations, as well as adaptive music and audio behaviors to control various characteristics of these sounds.

Once the configuration and testing of the audio is complete, the implementer can then build one or more sound banks with configuration information that the programmer can use to integrate the audio system with the rest of the game code. Commonly these banks and files can then be placed inside the game by the implementers in order to test them out within the game environment. In some cases, the game itself can be hooked to the middleware in real time. This is a great way to work, as it allows even faster design changes to be made on the fly.

Go to the Classroom in the App, and click on the Video screen to watch and hear more about the evolution of audio workflow in concept, as well as hands on FMOD tutorials.

THE OTHER SIDE OF THE FENCE—THE API

OK, let's look at what the programmer has to deal with when using middleware. Although the audio middleware system is constructed around a codebase, the programmer will rarely deal with it at that level. It's much more common for them to use an **API**, or Application Programming Interface. This is a set of instructions and script-based standards that allows access to the codebase without having to delve too deeply into the main code, which in some cases may not be accessible—in other words it may be what's called closed source. Web standards like HTML5, CSS, and JQuery are referred to as open source— you can look at their code. Open source is very popular, but may not be the best decision business-wise from a middleware developer.

A middleware company, like an audio tool development company, usually releases its API to the public so that other software developers can design products that are powered by its service. In some cases, they let people use it for free, like students and individuals for example. In other cases, they can charge both a use fee and licensing fee, depending. The trend is tending towards more freedom and openness in learning the tool, and only in the case of a commercial release is the license fee charged.

Not all audio engines are built the same. For many years, audio middleware was clunky, difficult both to use and understand. Over the years it has become much more user friendly with a strong concentration on ease of use and simplified workflow.

Current Middleware Tools

Let's take a very brief look at the commercial middleware products out there today. These are used mainly by small to mid-size independent game developers.

FMOD Studio

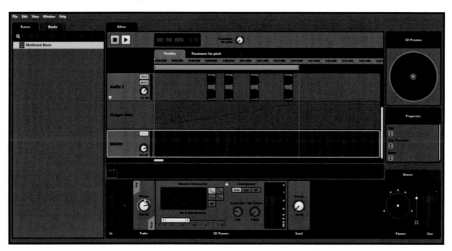

FMOD Studio.

Firelight Technologies introduced FMOD in 2002 as a cross platform audio runtime library for playing back sound for video games. Since its inception, FMOD branched into a low-level audio engine with an abstracted Event API, and a designer tool that set the standard for middleware editing/configuration reminiscent of DAWs. Firelight has since continued its innovation, releasing a brand new audio engine in 2013 called FMOD Studio with significant improvements over the older FMOD Ex engine, such as sample-accurate audio triggering, better file management, and a brand new advanced audio mixing system allowing busses, sends and returns.

Within the FMOD toolset a sound designer/implementer can define the basic 3D/2D parameters for a sound or event, in addition to the ability to effectively mock up complex parametric relationships between different sounds using intuitive crossfading and the ability to draw in automation curves and use effects and third-party plug-ins to change the audio. Music can also be configured within FMOD Studio using tempo based markers and timed triggers. The older FMOD Designer was among the first fully available toolsets that could be downloaded and used free for educational purposes. Additionally, due to their flexible licensing pricing structure, FMOD is now a solid and widely adopted audio middleware choice and continues to be a major player in today's game development environment.

Audiokinetic: Wwise

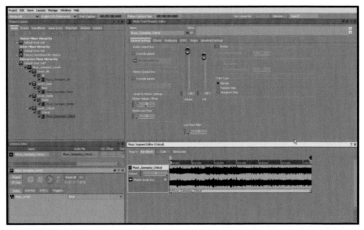

Wwise editor.

Introduced in 2006, the Wwise (Wave Works Interactive Sound Engine) and toolset provides access to features of their engine from within a staggeringly comprehensive content management UI. Their abstracted and modular Event system, which allows extremely complex and intricate results built from simple operations that can be nested within each other, has become a desired standard for many development houses worldwide. Wwise can configure events with the typical audio parameters expected of game audio middleware, with finely controlled randomization of volume, pitch, surround placement, and effects, as well as logic, switch/state changes, attenuation profiles and many more. The Interactive Music Engine in Wwise is highly regarded as well, enabling unique and unpredictable soundtracks from a small amount of existing music material.

Profiling is also a strong feature of Wwise. The ability to mock up every aspect of the engine's ability brings the toolset further into a full prototype simulation outside of the game engine. Their commitment to consistently providing new features and improvements, including a manageable upgrade strategy at the low level, adds to their adoption at several publishers and even larger developers over last few years.

Other Middleware of Note

While FMOD and WWise are the most frequently mentioned middleware apps used in game audio, there are a number of other tools available that are worth mentioning.

Tazman Audio/Fabric

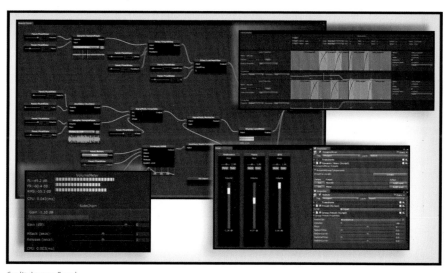

Credit: Jeremy Engel.

The Fabric toolset from Tazman Audio is yet another example of the changing dynamics of the game audio market. We've briefly mentioned the Unity3D game engine as a prominent force in today's game development world. Although Unity is based around the FMOD engine and API, there are very few features available to audio professionals to obtain middleware-like functionality without having to learn code in the process—as you will soon see in level 11. Fabric was created to address this situation at a very high and sophisticated level.

With an event-based system of triggering and sounds, plus randomized and sequenced backgrounds, parameter-based game mixing, and a modular-based effect building system, Fabric is becoming more and more a tool of choice for developers desiring a more high-level integrated tool inside Unity. Recently, however, Tazman Audio have signaled their intent to release the engine to work with a number of other game engines, which should be available sometime in 2014.

Miles Sound System

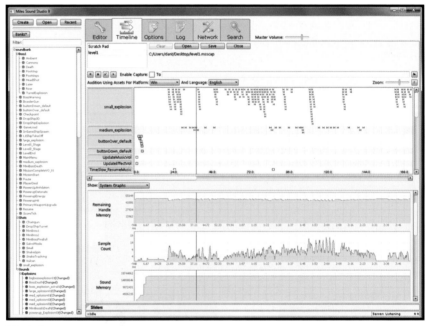

Miles Audio.

The Miles Sound System is one of the most popular pieces of middleware ever released. It has been licensed for over 5,000 games on 14 different platforms! Miles is a sophisticated, robust and fully featured sound system that has been around for quite some time—John Miles first released MSS in 1991 in the early days of PC gaming. Today, Miles features a toolset that integrates high-level sound authoring with 2D and 3D digital audio, featuring streaming, environmental reverb, multichannel mixing, and highly-optimized audio decoders. Along with all the usual encoding and decoding options, Miles uses Bink audio compression for its sound banks. Bink Audio is close to MP3 and Ogg in compression size, but is said to use around 30 percent less CPU than either.

Microsoft XACT and XAudio2

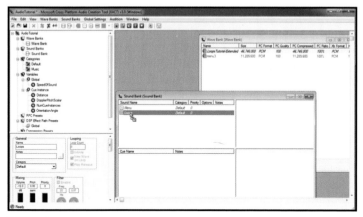

XACT in action.

Microsoft has taken great strides to provide audio tools to specifically leverage the features of its audio libraries, beginning with Direct Music Producer (see sidebar), and extending to the Xbox and Xbox 360 consoles in the form of XACT. Some of the standout additions to the engine and tool include the ability to author sound propagation curves, global variables including Doppler and speed of sound, real-time parameter control, and Reverb presets. Unfortunately Microsoft has since chosen to discontinue XACT (along with the free XNA game engine that it also supported) for both Windows 8 and the new Xbox One, leaving Microsoft-oriented developers and implementers with no graphically-based tools from the company to use.

However, the API that supports this new architecture, called XAudio2, is still going quite strong. Introduced in 2008 to replace DirectSound and XAudio, XAudio2 is a much more advanced audio library offering high-level performance. Significantly, it takes a somewhat more unique approach to sound generation by separating the sound data from its application in the mixing and processing setup. This means that multiple sounds can be potentially be mixed into a single stream, thus saving on CPU and memory. Another library called WASAPI (Windows Audio Session API) is beneficial for extremely low-latency 32-bit floating point audio, and is used primarily for middleware-oriented developers, rather than sound designers or game programmers.

Microsoft Direct Music Producer

Direct Music Producer, though primitive, was one of the first middleware applications regularly used in Windows games.

Based on the Microsoft Direct Music/ Direct Sound for PCs, the Direct Music Producer enabled interactive functionality using the features of the low-level audio libraries in Direct X. This included the ability to loop files, specify random or sequential playback behavior, create sample banks (DLS), and specify parameters for interactive playback using MIDI.

Conclusion

As we have seen in this level, middleware engines can give today's sound designer an amazing degree of control over how audio behaves and develops within a game environment. The first audio middleware programs were developed in-house and were the proprietary property of the companies that built them for specific uses within specific titles. That's still the case today, but over the years, third party companies have come along to provide audio engines and codebases for all sorts of platforms that did not have access to them before. Along the way the sophistication and power of these tools has significantly increased.

Nowadays, middleware puts a lot of this power directly into our hands, so we can make sure that the sound we are hearing in the game is exactly what's intended. Currently, if you are working on big budget titles you are much more likely to encounter audio middleware than if you are working on social or mobile games. This may change over time, as it always seems to, but where it will end up is anybody's guess.

Probably the best news for all of you budding game audio experts is that most of the software discussed in this chapter can be downloaded for free. And the free version is no different from the paid version. That makes exploring and bringing yourself up to speed on the latest middleware programs easy. Make no mistake about it, the use and understanding of audio middleware programs is one of the skills all game audio professionals should have readily available in their bag of tricks!

The Interactive Quiz for this Level is available in the App. In the main Classroom, click on the Quiz book to test your knowledge!

The Early Bird Gets the Worm
Preparing Your Audio

Mixing for Games

So, now that we have learned the basics of workflow concerning sound effects, music and voice-over, how do we go about preparing all of those awesome sounding assets for use in real live games? Well, you should have it hammered into your brain by now that we're dealing with non-linear media. Because of this the individual elements must be put into separate files and you will likely find yourself with folders and possibly subfolders of sounds. These asset folders need to be organized and properly named so that the game programmers can call the audio efficiently. This includes sound effects, individual music stems, voice-over and more. As discussed in previous Levels, there are a host of different requirements between genres of games that have a huge influence on how these audio elements will need to be organized. Ultimately, the answer to how they should be organized will emerge from the logic of the game itself.

Sometimes you may find yourself having to create multiple categories of sounds to accommodate your game and your team's needs.

Audio Preparation for Game Engines

Here are a few important workflow concepts to keep in mind when preparing your assets. You must . . .

- **Bounce out your sounds from a DAW** or Stereo Editor into individual files and into separate folders. These folders will contain all the music, sound effects and voice-over in the game and will need to be meticulously organized.
- **Tightly trim and edit your files** so that they can trigger right away when called by the game engine without skips or delay. We also need to trim the start and end of each sound so they are as size efficient as possible and don't take up any more space than is necessary. Game audio is all about efficiency.

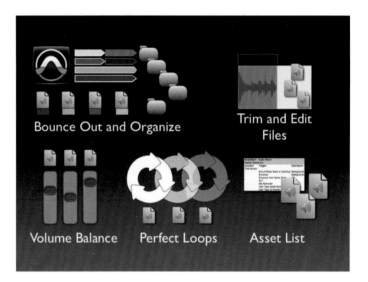

- **Volume balance all your audio.** In some cases you will normalize all your elements as individual groups (meaning for example all voice-over files) to 90 percent of maximum volume to prevent clipping, deliver them, and then let the programmers and integrators set the final mix volumes between these groups. In other situations you will premix the entire soundtrack in your DAW—this means you mix the sounds in your DAW, but bounce out the individual files or layers needed along with any reverb, EQ or effects you require and then deliver these files for insertion into the game. In this case, and with luck, the programmer will simply insert the files into the game with no need to do any additional audio work.

- **Create perfect seamless loops that do not skip**. We cannot stress this enough—there is nothing worse than getting audio notes that say "Sorry, but the audio is skipping. Can you please re-edit?" We'll have a lot more to say on the subject of looping later on in this level.

- **Provide an asset list or asset database management system** to properly identify your files so a programmer can help to implement them. Alternately, you would provide prepared audio middleware files or do the implementation yourself! Audio does not magically appear inside a game—it takes planning and elbow grease. If you don't know how to do it yourself, then you must make sure that at the very least you understand the process and can provide the programmer with the information they need to get the job done in as efficient a manner as possible.

Go to the Classroom in the App, and click on the Video screen to watch and hear more about preparing your audio for games!

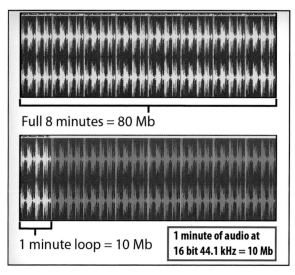

Full 8 minutes = 80 Mb

1 minute loop = 10 Mb

1 minute of audio at 16 bit 44.1 kHz = 10 Mb

This figure shows what should be pretty obvious by now—a looped file of 1 minute duration played eight times is much smaller in size than an 8 minute long file. This does not mean that all loops have to be short, however: these decisions are individual to the game and the situation at hand.
Credit: Jeremy Engels.

JUST SO YOU KNOW. . . .

Triple A console titles and big budget games usually involve the use of audio middleware. When a designer works with a middleware engine, all the audio elements are roughly balanced ahead of time, then the mix is refined in real time while the game is being played. Reverb or other effects can be added, music levels are frequently reduced in volume under voice-over through a process called ducking, and spatial sounds are all dealt with on the fly within the middleware audio engine. This is then output to the game engine itself or possibly to a platform-specific development environment like XCode, Visual Studio, or myriad others, to be compiled along with the graphic and structural game data.

Social and mobile games, like iOS, Android and online games, do not usually use audio middleware. In the case of platforms like these that don't use dynamic mixing, audio elements must be pre-balanced ahead of time by the sound designer, or balanced out by the programmer or designer within the game environment.

THE IMPORTANCE OF LOOPING IN GAMES

As you're painfully aware by this point, looping is a HUGE part of creating sound effects or music, primarily because of the open nature of time in gameplay. It is impossible to write a perfectly timed music cue when you have no idea how long a player will stay in a specific area within the game environment. Looping also saves space in the game—for example, having a 1 minute loop play eight times is vastly more efficient than having an 8 minute loop playing once. Do the math—the former only takes up 1 minute of audio data at a given bit and sample rate, with a command to repeat eight times, and the latter lasts for 8 minutes at the same bit and sample rate. In other words, it is eight times larger. The other factor to consider is that even at eight times the size, it may still not fill all the time necessary to fulfill the gameplay requirements. Looping audio in games is a global phenomenon that pertains to sound effects, music, and ambient backgrounds.

Uses for Looping Techniques

Sound Effects: A good example of a looping sound effect is a weapon effect in an FPS game, such as a machine gun. Holding down the appropriate button or firing key triggers the loop to play indefinitely (or perhaps until you run out of bullets), and when you release the button it can either stop, or more interestingly, trigger an ending sound (like a single shot or with shell casings clattering on the ground).

Ambient Backgrounds: Location loops are extremely common in games of all shapes and sizes. Outdoor locations or tailored indoor acoustic environments in general use longer audio clips in order to avoid a sense of repetition. One technique for developing a well-crafted loop might be to have the same audio material at the beginning and end, making it harder if not impossible for the ear to detect the loop point. Another technique is to use a few ambient loops of slightly differing length playing together, so that they overlap each other at different points. In this case, the goal is to try to make the game sound more organic and non-repetitive, while at the same time using smaller and more size-efficient files.

Music Soundtracks: In many games, producers want a lot of music, but just don't have the audio budget available for one reason or other. In such cases, looping is a necessary evil. We have all at one time or another become aware of a repetitive music score in a game—in fact, parents seem especially sensitive to such things! Repetition is necessary and sometimes it's even expected—*Space Invaders* or *Asteroids*, anyone? Even with today's sophisticated console games there are a ton of very clever techniques that are used to give the player a feeling that there is more music around then there really is. By cleverly changing or layering the orchestration in musical passages, composers are able to turn 30 minutes of music into stems that can run for over an hour without wearing out their welcome.

In certain styles of games, composers develop quick stinger effects to cover up transitions between gameplay or just to inject an unexpected quality into the game. In all cases, it is important to find out the time durations of the gameplay sections you will be composing for, and seek to provide music loops that will not become overtly repetitive. It also takes a highly skilled composer to know how much melody to include in looping musical passages. Too much and you may drive the listener bonkers, too little and there may not be enough tension or development to hold their attention. Similar to film music, often the best kind of loop is the one you don't even hear because it's so well integrated with the game.

Creating Perfect Loops

Creating suitable loops is an art form in itself. So now that you know how important looping is, how do you do it?

Looping often starts in a DAW. Loops are self-contained audio regions, that are sourced or recorded and then cut, trimmed and tested to make sure they do not skip. It is a good idea to test your loops in a stereo editing program like Sound Forge or Adobe Audition after you bounce them out of your DAW to make sure that your ear is not being fooled and that they are in fact seamless.

Be patient—sometimes it can take a while to find a seamless loop point, you may find yourself blowing up the waveform to quite an extreme degree in order to find a suitable zero crossing point. What's that? Well, a sound waveform graphically goes up and down around a center point of no volume. A seamless loop can most likely be created when the end of the loop and the beginning of the loop cross the exact center of the waveform where the volume of the wave is essentially zero. This is known as a "zero crossing" and it is vital to avoid clicks and pops. If you're only selecting a loop of a few waveform cycles you can visually see the beginnings and endings of loops easily on the screen. However, for longer loops you may need blow up the waveform view to a more extreme magnification. Then you will set your loop markers, listen, and gradually change your marker points until a suitable zero crossing is found.

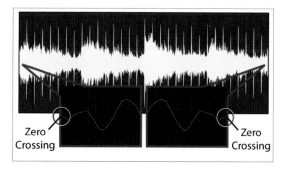

This image shows how to get a seamless loop by using a zero crossing to smooth the transition point between the beginning and end of the file. *Credit:* Jeremy Engels.

In some cases, it may be necessary to fade the waveform in or out, or you may also need to redraw the very end point of a wave file to avoid that pop or click. The length of the fade in/out will depend greatly on the situation. If you're trying to create the best example of a continuous fan hum or an ominous turbine sound in an engine room then you may be reducing the length of your fades to mere milliseconds in order to avoid an obvious sense of the sound fading in and out. In other cases, some effects may have a pulsing component where they rise and fall naturally or regularly and this can be taken advantage of when designing your loop. Loops can be tricky and sometimes it takes a little bit of practice to get them right, but it's really worth it to get it right before you send it out the door!

Audio Format Choices

When first deciding to take on any kind of work, you definitely must understand the limitations of your audio budget, and make decisions accordingly. In some cases this means the use of compressed audio. In previous levels we covered many different types of compression schemes, and each one has advantages and disadvantages. For example, MP3 encoding tends to ruin your carefully tailored seamless looping. Though there are various tools and strategies for dealing with these problems it may be more convenient, less labor intensive and show no quality difference to just use a different format.

Here is where knowing your operating systems and hardware limitations is extremely helpful. For example, if I'm creating sound for a PC/Mac web-based game and I'm having an issue with MP3 loops that skip, rather than trying to fix my MP3, I might simply switch to Ogg instead. However, I can't do that with an iOS game. I either have to solve my MP3 issue through coding or tools, or switch to an AAC based file. These are the kinds of educated decisions a game audio professional frequently has to make. So get used to keeping up on the latest and greatest formats and hardware and operating system capabilities!

Keep in mind that in some cases you may be asked to compress the files yourself, and in others you will deliver only uncompressed WAV or AIF (PCM) files and the programmer will deal with it. In the first case, you can use whatever commercial tools are available, such as a stereo audio editor, DAW or even iTunes or Windows Media. You may even be asked to use the tools provided by the game engine or platform to compress the sound files. In the second case, you need to be in touch with the producer or programmer and should be able to speak intelligently with them about the various compression schemes that are available and what the trade-offs may be, so you can help them to make the best decision as to which audio file format to use and what quality trade-offs they may experience as a result.

Conclusion

You can see that preparing your audio assets before putting them in the game is an absolute requirement if you want the results to sound professional. This can involve either basic normalizing or premixing your files before bouncing them. Interactivity changes the landscape of your audio workflow, and of how we think about mixing audio for games. The extra element of indeterminacy forces us to be prepared to have sound triggered in multiple ways and at a moment's notice. Now that you have a deeper understanding of how to prepare assets for use in a game engine, let's cover what a game engine actually IS. As you power up to the next Level, we'll cover in more detail how these engines are structured. We'll examine how they developed over time, and how they work to organize and trigger sounds and other media. See you there!

The Interactive Quiz for this Level is available in the App. In the Classroom, click on the Quiz book to test your knowledge!

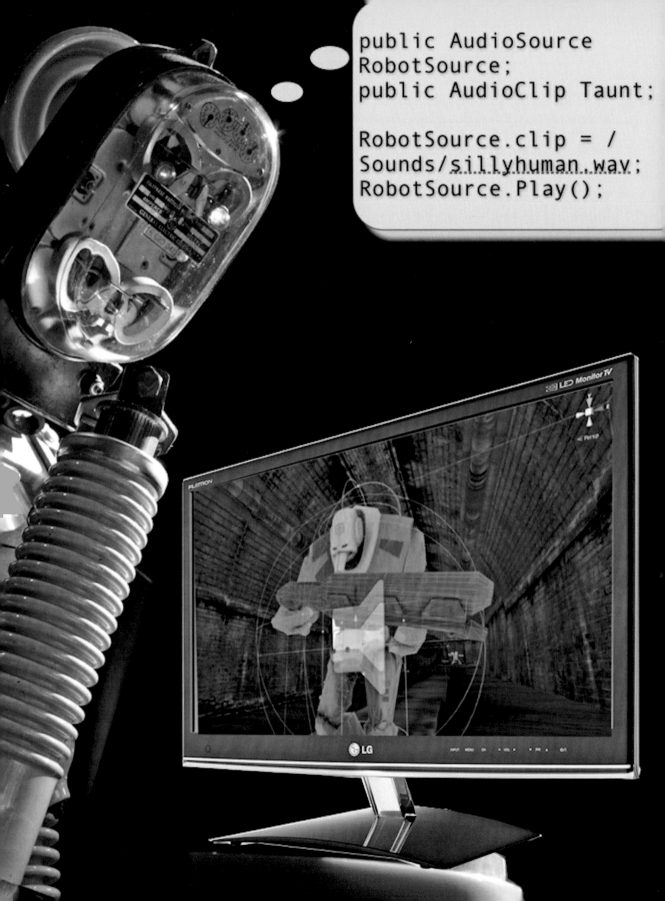

"Silly Human . . ."
How Game Engines Think

Background of Game Engines

Before game engines existed, games were usually written by programmers from scratch for specific platforms. Every time a new game was developed, the programmer largely had to start from the ground up and recode the entire game for that same platform. Remember, these first games were written to run on very limited resources, and would have to take maximum advantage of minimum materials in order for the game to run optimally. In addition, a game written for one particular platform would often have to be almost completely rewritten if it were ported to another platform, due to differences in hardware engendered by both competition and the rapid development of hardware capability in the field. This constant need to re-create the wheel over and over again became exceedingly onerous for game developers, and led directly to the development of game engines.

Standardization in Game Development

This difficult situation, in spite of the need for change, continued until the development and rise of the PC gaming market. PCs needed to have standards in which graphics, sound and controller input would conform to certain norms in order for computers to run a variety of applications consistently. The first jump toward standardization in game development took place in the graphics sector. A number of third-party developers began to create graphics engines, or what were called renderers, for use by game developers. These software drivers would do the hard work of interacting with a variety of different video cards. At the same time, it presented developers with a simplified set of common APIs that they could use to draw various game elements efficiently. The best known of these renderers, Reality Lab, became Direct3D after being purchased by Microsoft, which became the graphics-oriented component of the DirectX multimedia API, still in use today.

With the rendering standards of DirectX or OpenGL (which followed soon after Direct3D in the 1990s), the next step was to encompass other elements and functionality into a game-oriented development environment. The first-person shooter genre led the way in this case, specifically with the development of *Doom* by id Software. John Carmack designed a game engine which not only helped him create game levels and interaction for his game, it also led to him licensing his engine to other developers of similar titles such as *HeXen*, *Heretic*, and *Strife*. These developers used the *Doom* engine, but developed their own characters, rules, weapons, sounds and levels. In other words, all the content was developed by them, but the framework in which this content would function was licensed from a competitor.

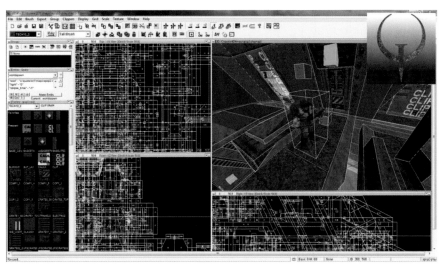

This image shows a popular *Quake* map editor called BSP. Though long out of publication, *Quake* is still popular with a number of dedicated gamers.

This trend increased in both complexity and intensity with the release of the *Quake* engine, developed for the game of the same name, also written by John Carmack. By this point other developers were beginning to see the revenue possibilities in game engine development, and competitors started to appear. In 1998, Epic Games released the game *Unreal*, which was created using their in-house development engine called, appropriately, the Unreal Engine. These engines further separated the roles of content and game design from each other, allowing development of game 'mods' such as the wildly popular *Counterstrike*. Modding, as it came to be known, enabled the average player to adapt and change game content to create their own unique variations. Other innovations included the development of a client and server model that greatly assisted with development of multiplayer and MMORPG games.

Current Game Engines

On the next page are a few selected game engines worthy of note, besides Unity 3D, the one we'll be looking at in more depth in the next levels. This is just a sampling and is by no means to be considered definitive in scope.

STRUCTURE OF A GAME ENGINE

So how does a game engine work, and how does it manage to keep track of all of those jillions of assets it has to deal with? Well, modern game engines are some of the most complex applications written, featuring dozens of finely tuned subsystems that leverage existing technology or tools oriented to specific areas of game design. Examples of these include lighting, sound, game physics, rendering, and asset control. All of these subsystems interact to ensure a precisely controlled and consistent playing experience. The continued evolution of game engines has created a strong separation between these various areas of design. It is not uncommon, for example, for a game development team to have several times as many artists as actual programmers. Using a game engine makes development of sequels much easier and faster, as the existing framework and content can be modified as needed.

A game engine is based on the concept of an IDE or Integrated Development Environment. IDEs are commonly used to create standard applications that run on your desktop or laptop. Xcode is the IDE used for Mac, iPhones, and iPads. Visual Studio is common for PC development. Eclipse is a popular IDE for developing Android applications. All of these use various data elements arranged in a specific hierarchy, often with libraries of commonly used functions for user input, video, sound, and more. However, because a game engine involves specific requirements, the design is generally different and more focused.

A typical 3D game engine can usually do the following:

- **Import and arrange pictures and 3D graphic models**. As we mentioned earlier, a game engine is usually not the place where items like 3D graphic models and 2D images are edited but it IS the place where they are imported, assembled together and their relationships are defined.
- **Import and arrange sound files**. As with graphics, game engines usually do not feature the ability to create or edit sound content. That task is usually left to a dedicated audio editing application such as Pro Tools or another DAW. The engine concerns itself mainly with HOW and WHEN the sound is used in the game interactively, not the specific sounds used.
- **Render light or edit objects**. Objects brought into the environment of the engine must be viewed accurately and, if necessary, modified in terms of texture, shape, or size. This is where DirectX or OpenGL support (many engines support both) is vital to the proper viewing of the objects or surfaces. Lighting is an essential dynamic element to any visual object—when a character in a game walks past this object, the light is dynamically changing. Arranging light sources, their intensity and position, will greatly affect how the game is viewed by the player. Texture is another useful two dimensional component, lending realism to a 3D surface making it look dingy or sparkling. The texture is usually a simple picture of real or imaginary surfaces, which are then mapped onto 3D models.
- **Determine the function of physics in the game**. The broad category of physics in games is hugely important and mainly deals with three things: **gravity**, which dictates how objects obey physical laws as well as laws of acceleration and momentum; **rotation**, which controls the angle of an object based on these rules; and **collision detection**. Of these three, collision detection is the most important to interactivity in a game environment, because it's the game engine's way of knowing when a physical object has touched or passed through another object. Physics governs

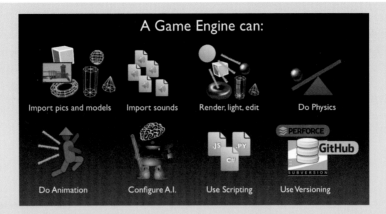

how realistically an element or asset in the game will perform within the "real world" of the game environment. This goes for complex things like particles in an explosion, as well as the rigidity of the material on an object.

- **Animation of objects**. Related to the concept of physics is animation. This field covers the area of objects moving under their own power, and not because of the laws of physics. Individual simple model animation can be imported from other designing programs that can handle it, but the overall interactions on a large scale of things like cars, other non-player characters, etc., is at least partially determined by animation movements. A typical animation in a game is when doors open between rooms due to a trigger action. The door's position is animated, and the animation starts when the trigger is activated due to a collision event received from the physics system.

- **Artificial Intelligence (AI)**. This broad category refers to the way in which objects in the game "think" and react to stimuli provided by the player. Mostly it is a set of rules governing behavior and strategy of the game's different elements depending on what the player does in the game. These behaviors can be very simple or very complex and interrelated to trigger points or goals achieved or unachieved. A simple example might be if a player passes a certain number of trigger points, then the amount of enemies will increase, or perhaps they will all move faster. Possibilities are many and AI is a vital part of what makes the game interesting, especially when playing against the computer.

- **Scripting**. This ability is akin to the glue that holds everything together in a game. Scripts govern the behavior of how objects will relate to one another based on certain conditions or criteria. This is where a rule like "Player cannot enter area X unless they possess object Y" would be created as well as the ability to override certain default settings within the application or to extend functionality with plug-ins. Actions like having a player run into something that makes a sound is governed by a script. Scripts are more often written in simplified structural forms like Javascript and its many variants, Python, or Lua, making it much easier than coding rules and behavior in C, C# or C++ though most well-known engines will support this kind of extensibility.

- **Asset control**. This means keeping track of all the items in a game, whether they are textures, 3D models, sounds, surfaces, AI behaviors, animations, rules, etc. Anything in a game has the potential to be reused at any time, so every element needs to be tracked, organized and categorized. Game engines can do this to some extent but sometimes extra help is needed, so for that, dedicated software may be needed to provide that extra level of security. An important subset of this is called version control, and occurs especially in situations where a version of a game section is perhaps updated while others are not. It's important to make sure every revision is compatible with the previous code and for that purpose, dedicated version control software such as Perforce or the open source Git or SVN can be helpful in these situations. There are many other things that game engines can do, but these are the most significant ones that pertain to our discussion of the game development world.

Unreal Engine

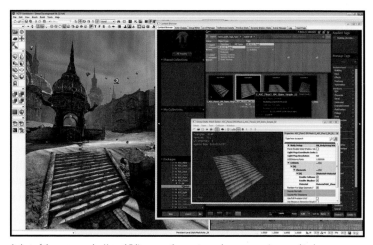

A shot of the very popular Unreal Editor, one the most popular game engines used today.

Although Unreal was developed for use on PC and console games, it has made some inroads to mobile through its free-to-download multiplatform development kit, the UDK (Unreal Developers Kit). The combination of a well-seasoned development toolset and a visual scripting interface makes it a good choice for many developers, but there is currently no Mac version of the editor.

CryEngine

An engine bred for extremely high FPS gaming performance on PC and console platforms. The SDK and editor tools are free to download and use for non-commercial purposes, but again the editor software is only for Windows.

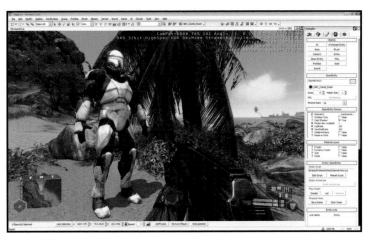

CryEngine's specialty is in creating high performance FPS games, with incredible graphics.

Stencyl

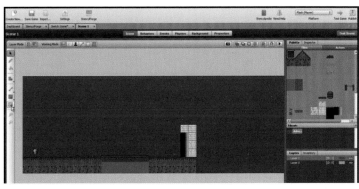

Stencyl is a popular tool for students and early developers making simple 2D games.

This is a well-constructed 2D game engine with a clean interface, helpful visual programming/scripting setup, and with Flash, iOS and Android support, popular on mobile for creating simple games. Originally an Actionscript-derived Flash engine, it's been transitioning into an HTML5 friendly engine. Stencyl runs equally well on Macs and PCs and is free to download for creating Flash based games.

Cocos2D-iPhone

This is a very popular free and open source development engine for iOS devices, based on Objective-C instead of the original Python of Cocos2D.

155

BounceMe is an example of the types of 2D-based games made with the Cocos-2D engine.

This engine is extremely coding intensive—there is no integrated editor to speak of, but as such, Mac, PC, and even Linux programmers can develop games using it.

Codea (iOS)

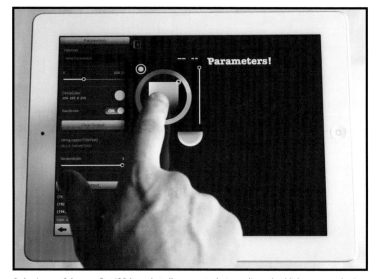

Codea is one of the very first iOS Apps that allows you to design, edit, and publish games to the App Store entirely on the iPad.

Just for fun, you can test your knowledge of **game engines** by going to the App Classroom, and clicking on the Word Search book!

Although extremely new, Codea is a totally self-contained game engine running exclusively on an iPad. The developers behind Codea create a touch-friendly development environment with scripting code, plus useful editing and testing tools that enable you to change parameters while playing. You can even publish your creations to the App Store!

For a larger list of game engines, check out the App, but be advised, engines come and go in popularity and there are literally hundreds out there.

How a Game Engine Thinks About Sound

Now that you have your assets designed, mixed and mastered, how do you get them into the game? And how do you deal with making them play once they're in there? The most important thing to keep in mind is that the logic behind a game engine is a computer's logic for the most part, but tailored to how that individual game is structured. In other words, a lot of that decision making is effectively out of your hands—you have to work within the limitations that you're given.

Keep in mind we all work with computers and machine logic every day. We use DAWs and other programs in order to make music and to design sounds. And we all have to deal with the limitations of what the tools can do. Limitations are a fact of life and game engines are no exception.

As far as getting the sound into the game—audio files are regarded by a game engine as an asset, essentially no different from any other asset, in basic principle. Most game engines will have one central area where all of the assets are stored—this is usually some kind of folder or directory. In order for the game to use the asset it generally has to be in the directory. In high-level development studios with a lot of team members, the directory will likely reside on a central server and the assets will be copied to it. In these cases version management through a tool like Perforce will be almost mandatory—with so many team members working on the game submitting changes, the ability to revise stable changes to the codebase becomes essential.

Getting the sound into the game can depend on a lot of factors. Probably the most obvious question is whether you need to be concerned with doing the importing of the sound in the first place. So let's say you are tasked with this importing—the next real obstacle is whether you can. Many game engines (especially for 2D games) are actually almost completely code based and have no editor to speak of outside of their IDE of choice or a common text editor. Thus putting the sound in the game in that case is literally copying the sound to the main directory or subdirectory of the game project. The game code then has to know where exactly these files reside (in technical terms applicable to coding this is called the filepath).

The remaining category is the more GUI-driven game IDEs like UDK and Unity, and here you can easily import an asset of any kind, including sound files. Once imported you may be able to use the game engine to adjust qualities of assets depending on your design desires. For example, is your sound a sound effect or a music file? Is it regarded as a 3D sound or a 2D one? Do you want to compress the sound in the engine? And so on . . .

Once these questions are answered we need to move into how the sound is triggered, and here we have to get at least a bit into naming conventions again. This is the common ground here—what you call the sound file is extremely important to a programmer, and the codebase might be organized in a very specific way. For example, let's say you organize your sounds by what room they happen in, but the programmer or designer organizes them by the particular sound bank they are associated with. Unless a lot of useful communication between these parties has been worked out beforehand as to the naming and other criteria, the result can be chaotic, requiring a lot of frustrating last minute reconfigurations that will not make anyone happy.

Once everything's in place inside the game itself, the process then goes to the testing and QA phase, which we already mentioned earlier is an integral and vital part of the process of getting a game designed and refined.

The Importance of Testing and Design Iteration

Subjecting a game to testing and QA (Quality Assurance) is probably one of the most vital things to prepare for when designing sound for a game. Testing of course can uncover bugs in the code and playability, but more important, it shows you exactly how your work sounds inside the game and whether there are artistic or technical issues you will need to redesign or adjust. For example, you might make some awesome high energy music for a game's user interface menu and then realize as you're playing it that the music is just too cluttered and busy and actually takes away from the playing experience. Remember, in games, form follows function—our job is to serve the game and work with, not against, the platform. It's definitely important to get feedback from the designer and producer as well, but don't just wait for their feedback—be proactive in making your audio the best it can be for that situation by playing the game.

Design iteration, which is becoming a popular term, means that you continue to adjust and modify design of a product based on any number factors—tester feedback, concept changes, gameplay balance, etc. Iteration means to repeat something, so in this case the audio design is altered, then tested, refined again and re-tested, and so on. For you, this can mean changes to the game's entire look and feel or just simple refinements to enhance playability.

Stay flexible in your expectations—these changes may be big, requiring to you to essentially start over again with all new content, or they may just involve simple tweaks to existing content. From the sudden realization that the bass from your awesome dubstep bass drop doesn't hit quite as hard on a tiny iPad speaker, to sounds that seem to be out of sync with simple animations, even though you are absolutely sure you

The Interactive Quiz for this Level is available in the App. In the Classroom, click on the Quiz book to test your knowledge!

had them perfectly timed in your studio, in the game testing and QA world things are going to change, and being open to iteration is just part of the landscape.

Conclusion

Well, we've covered a great deal of ground here in our understanding of game engines. Once you import a sound, it can't be edited within the App, because that's not generally how a game engine works. An audio file is not much different from any other asset in a game—it's just an external file that's triggered by the code. There are some behaviors that can be defined, such as compression, streaming options, or 3D and 2D settings, but none of these actually alter the original source file permanently. Once in the game, the next process is to create testable versions and listen to how your sound and music assets are working (or not), and to exchange feedback with the game's team members to determine how to improve, revise, or change your sounds so that the result will be a smooth and fluid game experience. This is called design iteration and is part of nearly every game's development process. In this phase you'll also be trying to push your game to see how all the systems perform under stress, which is useful for ensuring your sound triggering is accurate, robust and reliable.

In our next level, we will crack open the hood of the very popular game engine, Unity 3D, and show you what makes it tick and how its inner logic works, with special focus on the audio system and how to configure it for both music and sound effects.

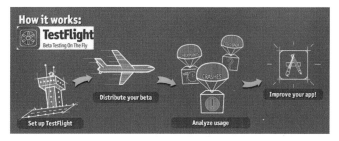

This image shows the basic process used in Testflight, one of the most popular beta testing services for iOS and Android.

Testflight

The Testflight tool was developed in 2010, and helped streamline a process for testing iOS devices that was somewhat complicated. Before Testflight was launched, the only way to test a game on an iOS device was to get its unique identification number, or UDID. Once discovered (a process that could be somewhat involved), a tester would submit the UDID number to the programmer who would then contact the manufacturer (Apple in this case) to get permission to download the application to that particular device. Although different third-party tools appeared to smooth that process out, Testflight has created a convenient, well-managed system with their website communicating with the device, enabling it to send its UDID automatically. It also makes it possible for developers to set up multiple accounts using these same device IDs, and be able to send or update builds to multiple users at the click of a button. In addition, it now supports Android devices as well, so that the vast majority of mobile developers can take advantage of its convenience.

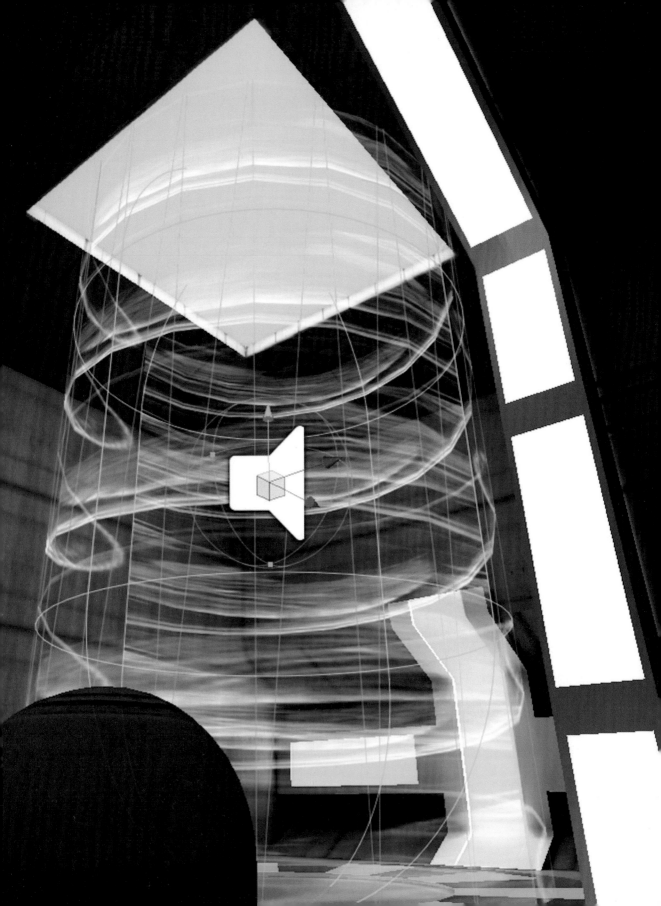

Unify My World
Audio in Unity 3D

Getting Familiar With Unity's Structure

This award-winning game development engine is a relative newcomer to the game engine field, starting in 2005 with the first version emerging after 4 years of development, debuting at Apple's WWDC (World Wide Developer Conference). By 2007 they had launched version 2 of the

Unity logo.

software which had support for console development on the Nintendo Wii. In 2008 they announced iPhone support for the program, one of the first engines to do so. By 2009 they were offering a free fully functional trial version for educational and non-commercial purposes, and by 2010 they had 250,000 developers registered. In fall of that year they released the redesigned version of Unity 3D, and as of this writing there are now well over two million registered developers using Unity 3D.

There are two versions of Unity 3D. The free version is called Unity Free or Unity Basic while the paid version is Unity Pro. Both flavors of Unity can be downloaded for free with a limited timed trial license for Unity Pro. Presently, the differences in terms of features between Unity and Unity Pro are fewer than most Free and Pro program combinations. For a complete list of the differences check out the Unity website www.unity3d.com.

Version 4 brought significant improvement in look and feel plus extended support for more platforms and scripting.

Platform Development Support

Here's a basic list of the supported platforms as of this publishing:

- Mac/Linux Desktop application
- PC Desktop application (including Windows 8 support)
- Web Player (HTML 4,5/Javascript based, requires downloadable plug-in)
- Nintendo Wii and Wii U
- PlayStation 3, Playstation Vita, Playstation 4
- Xbox 360, Xbox One
- iOS (iPod Touch, iPhone, iPad)
- Android OS
- Windows Phone and Windows 8 Mobile

UNITY'S AUDIO ENGINE: UNDER THE HOOD

As with a lot of game engines the Unity developers chose to use an existing middleware audio toolset in order to generate sounds in game. Unity's audio duties are thus handled by an older version of the FMOD audio engine (which you should be familiar with from earlier levels), and inherit a lot of terminology from it as well. Unlike the full version of FMOD though, Unity only comes with a basic low-level access to the FMOD Ex API, and Unity's programmers have implemented only a portion of its more advanced functionality and almost none of its GUI-based features. Access to these FMOD-derived features in Unity (beyond the basics, which we'll be covering) is usually done in code via Unity's API, based around a C# code interface (with a couple of shorthand scripting variants). While the API uses a few FMOD terms, it does not resemble FMOD code or scripting in any significant way.

To be clear, this means that there is currently no direct support for FMOD Designer functionality in Unity. However, there are a few third party methods that allow some features of FMOD Designer to be used within Unity, as well as some tools that offer middleware-like features. In addition, Unity's older FMOD Ex based audio engine can itself be replaced by a different one through the use of plugins. These are described in the paragraph below.

Extending Unity's Engine: Supported Audio Formats

Like quite a few other game engines, Unity Pro also supports the use of plug-ins. These provide more or alternate functionality than can be provided through the C# scripting interface. This extends to audio engines as well. Both Audiokinetic's Wwise and FMOD Studio (the newest version of FMOD) have now some level of integration available in Unity's Editor. This essentially bypasses Unity's own audio engine, replacing it with the plugin's version. It must be noted that this integration is very low level, however—you'll have to trigger any Wwise or FMOD Studio events completely through code or scripting from Unity.

Supported audio formats for Unity include:

- **Uncompressed Audio support**: Unity supports WAV and AIFF, the two most common audio formats in use today.
- **Compressed Audio Support**: Unity supports both import and playback of MP3 and Ogg Vorbis files. Ogg files are supported in desktop applications (Mac, PC and Linux) while MP3 files are supported on import for all platforms.
- **Modtracker Support**: Unity supports four formats of Modtracker files which offer incredibly compressed file sizes (these are actually MIDI files combined with compressed sample data, made popular in the nineties).
- **Audio Encoding**: Unity can encode uncompressed audio into Ogg Vorbis for desktop applications, and uses MP3 for mobile applications due to the presence of hardware decoders that support it.

Support for Filtering/Effects

Because Unity uses FMOD's audio capabilities, it does come with a lot of extra DSP-oriented features. These features are mainly only supported in the Pro version and include the following:

- Low Pass Filter
- High Pass Filter

- Echo Filter
- Distortion Filter
- Chorus Filter
- Reverb Filter
- Reverb Zone (Pro and Free)

HOW SOUND WORKS IN UNITY

The basic principle of sound in Unity is determined by two Game Object Components—the Audio Listener and the Audio Source. Both of these components work in combination with the sound file itself. You can think of the Audio Listener as you—or, more specifically, as your ears, or perhaps a microphone—while the Audio Source is, as you might expect, the source of the audio, which can be any object in the game world.

Audio Listener

The Audio Listener Component is usually attached to a first- or a third-person controller combined with a camera (which represents your eyes or your view of yourself). An Audio Listener is necessary only if the sound functions within a three-dimensional environment; it is not generally needed for a two-dimensional game. Unity limits you to only one Audio Listener.

Audio Source

The Audio Source Component is just that, a source of audio in the game world. Audio sources can be set up to play 2D or 3D sounds in a variety of ways. One way is a simple ambient background that loops. You've already heard examples of this in the *Mushroom Forest* game environment we covered in a previous level.

If the Audio Source is attached to an object and plays continuously, distance from the object is important in the game, and the volume settings of the Audio Source can be customized to a wide variety of settings based on the distance. Audio Filters, if available, can also be employed by this same method, enabling more realistic depictions of occlusion and obstruction.

Triggering an Audio Source

An Audio Source can be triggered by a number of conditions, but only a very few of them can be configured using no coding or scripting expertise. The simplest of these is an object appearing in the game space for the first time. The sound is tied to the source by a sound trigger, and looping can be turned on or off as well.

Any other type of triggering will require some scripting knowledge and usage of other components. For example, an object might make a sound if the player runs into it. The object will not play the sound on its own, however; the sound requires the trigger event, which in this case is the collision, and the direction to play a sound comes from the script. Another example would be a sound that occurs when you click on the mouse to fire in a first-person shooter. In this case, a script is set up to look for mouse events, so when a mouse event is detected, the script triggers the sound to play.

Hands On With Unity

In order to give you a better idea of how audio sources can function and be triggered inside a game environment, you really need to understand at least a little bit about how Unity is put together. We're going to take you step-by-step through Unity to help you re-create an extremely simple game function. A player will walk around a simple virtual environment with an ambient background and walk into an object, which will make a sound of some kind. In the process you'll learn at least a little bit about how Unity itself works and begin to understand the logic underlying its engine.

To continue, you'll need to download Unity and install it first. Open a web browser and go to **www.unity3d.com/downloads**. This might take a bit of time, as the installer is about 1GB in size. Go watch a movie, or have a sandwich while it downloads. Once you've downloaded and installed the program, go to the following website to get our free basic demo level

READ ME!

While we recommend downloading and trying our demo example project from the website (www.focalpress.com/cw/Horowitz) we understand that readers may be confused and bewildered by a lot of seemingly non-audio related material. Also some people may have some technical limitations that preclude them from downloading and installing new software. Don't panic! This is all very useful knowledge and we've done our best to accommodate different learning methods. Here are your available options:

1. Download a working Unity demo: You can download Unity and then download our simple demo project from the Focal Press website at www.focalpress.com/cw/Horowitz, and follow along in the book with the procedures outlined on the next page.
2. If you cannot or do not wish to download the demo, or you need further assistance, go to the application and check out the Unity walkthrough in the Holodeck area.

Go to the main classroom in the App, and click on the Videos screen to watch the step-by-step tutorials covering Unity's basic structure.

Interact with a dynamic 3d environment created in Unity, by going to the Holodeck area in the App or by using this URL www.focalpress.com/cw/Horowitz

project file (www.focalpress.com/cw/Horowitz). Download that zip file and uncompress it into its folder and we'll be ready to go.

Getting To Know the Unity Interface: Hands On

I'll start off by saying that this is one complex program to use for sure, and we are only going to look at the barest essentials that specifically relate to importing and adding sounds within the program. It's extremely deep, but that being said, the sound part is relatively easy to deal with.

Let's open up Unity. On a PC you will find it under C: (or it may also be 'My Computer') \Program Files\Unity. On a Mac its normal location is in the /Applications/Unity folder on your hard disk. Open this folder and double click the App to start it up. If this is your first time starting up Unity you'll be presented with a registration screen. You can either register online or take the registration key to another machine that is connected to the Internet. The basic download of the game comes with a free license and an option for activating the limited demo of the Unity Pro version. You will also see the Welcome to Unity window giving you links to various Tutorials, videos, documentation, and the forum.

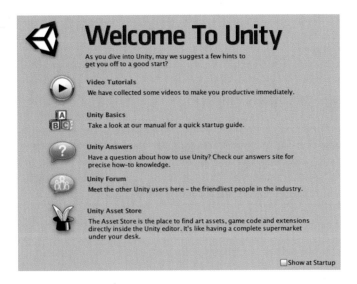

Anatomy of a Unity Project

If you close the Welcome screen what you will be looking at is a Unity Project in the Unity Editor. Most likely you will be looking at the demo project that comes with Unity. While it's pretty cool to look at, there are a lot of objects in it and it may get a bit confusing. So let's strip things down and give you a somewhat simpler project I modified, courtesy of the Unity Asset Store and Mixed Dimensions.

Go to the **File** menu and choose **Open Project**. In the window that opens, you'll see the list of recently opened projects (which should be largely empty). We want to open a new Project, so choose **Open Other** to load a Unity Project and navigate to wherever you saved the folder you downloaded from the book's website at www.focalpress.com/cw/ Horowitz. In most cases this will be in the /Users/(*username*)/Downloads folder on a Mac, or on the PC it's usually under C:\Users\(username)\ Downloads. When you have found this folder just click **Open** on the folder itself—you don't need to go into the folder to find a file. Let this file open up, and we'll be ready to go!

NOTE: If Unity gives a warning that it's going to update the project and you can't go back to an earlier version, this is normal, as Unity is updating fairly frequently. Just choose the **OK** or **Continue** button to move ahead.

Unity project structure.

The Project is the largest file structure available in Unity. Everything in Project goes into a master folder with the project's name. This means all of your tangible game assets, as well as all other kinds of utility files and stored settings. The analogy of a project is that it is basically your whole game. Copying the entire Project folder will effectively duplicate your game, and is a good idea as a backup plan, should your original Project folder get corrupted. The keyword here is *permanent*. The Project is a place for things you will use in the game and they generally won't be deleted or altered in any way.

A VIEW TO YOUR PROJECT

Unity organizes the contents of your project visually into what are called **Views**. These are extremely flexible—you can adjust boundaries on any View by dragging its edges around the screen and it will resize accordingly. Additionally any View can easily be maximized by simply mousing over its tab (you don't have to click) and pressing the spacebar. The maximized View can then be toggled to return back to its original size by pressing the spacebar again. Try it out—it's fun! Each View has its name printed clearly on its Tab. There are a quite a few of these, but we'll be covering the **Project**, **Hierarchy**, **Scene Inspector** and **Game Views** in this level.

To get ourselves on the same visual page as it were, look in the far upper right corner of the main editor for the **Default** label. The Default layout is the Hierarchy View on the upper left, Scene/Game Views in the top center, the Inspector View on the right side, and the Project and Console Views on the bottom left and bottom center. This is what is indicated in the screenshot.

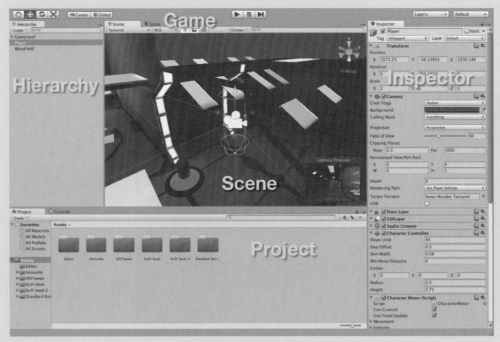

This screenshot shows the placement of Views in the Default Layout. Views can be customized to suit your needs and preferences, and you can save and recall Layouts as well.

Let's check out the Project View first. The most common part of any Unity project that you will be dealing with is the **Assets** folder, found directly under the main project folder in the View. The Assets folder contains all of the aforementioned tangible things like 3D models, textures, scripts and of course, sound files. To import assets into a project, you will generally be dealing with this View. Doing so will make a copy of the asset, which is the recommended method. You can also add things like scripts and folders to the Project as well as many other things, but we need to be moving on. Let's talk about the **Scene** file.

The Scene

Significantly, the Project's Assets folder will contain at least one **Scene** file. The Scene is where all of the less tangible things take place in a game. The keyword to think of here is *temporary*. A Scene file is similar to a single game level in a game. In the Scene environment things become less tangible and more virtual in nature. Opening up a Scene file will display its contents in the Hierarchy View as a name and also visually inside the Scene View.

One thing you may notice is that when we opened the Project we ended up in an **Untitled Scene**. If you look at the contents of the Hierarchy View in the upper left side and the Scene View you'll see that they will only have a **Main Camera** object in them and nothing will appear in the Scene or Game Views. We need to open a Scene file, so look for the file called **TestSound-SciFi.unity** in the Assets folder in the Project View and double click that. Now that we've done so, we can see the list of objects on the left and the visual representation of our game space just to the right side in the center in the Scene View.

It's extremely important to point out here that these Objects in a Scene can change constantly. For example, if I'm playing the game and shoot a robot and it explodes, the Robot Game Object is removed from the Scene. Or if suddenly a dozen magic fireballs appear and flame out, this means they get created, go through their animation and then get deleted. The Scene is a totally dynamic place where anything can happen (and usually does).

The Game Object

This is the virtual building block of a Scene. Everything listed in the Hierarchy View you're looking at is a **Game Object**. These can be physically visible inside the game space, or they can be invisible. Every Game Object possesses characteristics and/or behaviors. Unity refers to each of these specific behaviors as **Components**.

The Component

Click on any object in the Hierarchy to see these Components on the right side in the Inspector View.

Every Game Object in a Scene will have at least one Component called a **Transform** (which governs every object's position, size, and rotation), and more Components can be added.

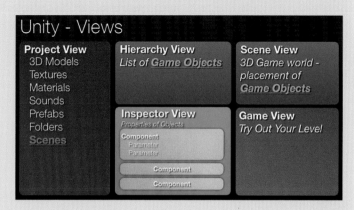

169

Some Components are predefined, and others can be customized, such as scripts. Components will have various settings or parameters associated with them and these of course can change. To do audio in Unity you will also need to add Components (the aforementioned Audio Listener and Audio Source).

So that's the basic structure in a nutshell—the Project contains all your real assets, including Scene files, which contain virtual Game Objects. These in turn contain Components that define the behavior of a particular object. Now let's examine how all of these Game Objects in a Scene are visually represented by getting into Scene View.

Moving Around in the World

Scene View

This is where the vast majority of graphic editing and arranging is done for objects within Unity (although Unity is not a graphic editor, remember that!). Let's examine the objects in the Scene—if you take a look on the left side you'll notice fairly few Game Objects, and the visual material in our Scene view is equally sparse. You have a terrain, a wall, a player object and a sphere representing a basic Audio Source.

Now in this window your view is controlled by the camera, which you can zoom, pan and rotate. Since navigating areas of a scene in Unity is pretty vital to being able to select objects in the scene, let's go over the ways we can control our view.

There are a lot of methods but I find the most usable way is to have a two-button mouse or to have a right-click set up on laptops that have multi-touch trackpads. This enables **Flythrough Mode**, and at this point you can use keyboard keys to navigate through the scene.

First, though, locate the Toolbar section on the top left—it should look like this:

Click on the **Hand** object to select the **Camera Move** mode, then right-click (you cannot use Control-click for this, there has to be a dedicated right-click option) and hold.

As you are holding, you have entered Flythrough mode, and the Hand tool should turn into an Eye, and the cursor in the screen should also be changed to an eye.

Now you can efficiently navigate through the scene. Using the mouse you can change view and pan rotation similar in a manner used by RTS

games. You can use this now to change angle and elevation with the addition of the following keys:

- W   Zooms into the scene
- S   Zooms back out of the scene
- A   Tracks camera to the left
- D   Tracks camera to the right
- E   Tracks camera up
- Q   Tracks camera down

You can use the mouse or trackpad plus the Hand tool to move around the scene as well, and there are alternate controls, which you can use if these don't work or you're really curious:

- Use the arrow keys to move around on the X and Z axes
- X Axis (left/right, with the left and right arrows)
- Z Axis (forward/back with the up-arrow forward and the down-arrow back)
- Hold Option/Alt and click-drag to orbit the camera around the current pivot point
- Hold Option/Alt and middle click-drag to drag the Scene View camera around. You need a three-button mouse (or trackpad shortcut) for this.
- Hold Option/Alt and right click-drag to zoom the Scene View. This is the same as scrolling with your mouse wheel or using the W and S keys in Flythrough.

One extremely important thing to do is to be able to center your view on something you've selected. So, once you have found the object you want to select, click on it and press the F (Frame) key with the cursor in the Scene View. This will center the Scene View and pivot point on the selection.

Help, I'm Lost In Space!

We've all been there. Suddenly your camera is pointing towards some random direction and you're totally lost. So another extremely nifty thing, is that if you know the name and location of a Game Object in the Hierarchy, you can click on it, hover the mouse within the Scene View (don't click in the Scene View, as this could potentially select another object), press F and the view will instantly zoom to that object and center it in the view.

OK—Take a few minutes and try flying through the scene using the controls mentioned here.

Game View

We have one more important view to discuss and that's Game View. This View is, as you might guess, the view that is active when playing the game or Scene itself. It is inactive until you start the Scene using the playback controls at the top center of the Edit View.

When you click the Play arrow, the arrow turns blue and Game View becomes active. If you click the Maximize on Play button on the right side of the Scene View, the game will be played in the maximum screen space possible. In the Game View, you can use many of the controls you used in Flythrough mode (the mouse and the W, A, S, and D keys), but you cannot use the up and down controls (Q and E). You can also use the left and right arrows to track left or right (without turning), and the up and down arrows to move forward or back.

If your screen is not maximized, you can select and edit objects in the Hierarchy, Scene and Project while you play the game. However, there is a very important point to make if you do this. ALL objects in the Hierarchy and Scene Views will revert to their original states when you stop playing the game (including deleting Objects). The Project View will remain unaffected however. So, if you want changes you make to be permanent, you should make changes to assets in the Project View, and not in the Scene Hierarchy View. If you have to remember a change to an Object in the Scene View, taking a screenshot of your Inspector settings is a convenient way to do this. To turn Game View off, simply click the Play arrow again to disable playback.

So now that we've covered this, click the Play button at the top, and play your scene. Walk around using the keyboard keys and mouse/trackpad, and notice the various things in the environment. You won't hear any sound in the project though, because we haven't yet associated any sound files or created any Audio Sources.

Conclusion

As you can see, the Unity game engine is an extremely deep, complex, and involved environment to create games, and we have barely even begun to scratch the surface as to what's possible here. Whether you are just using the App or if you are getting your hands dirty with our demonstration level, at this point, you should have a solid grasp of the basic sound functionality that is available within Unity. You should also know how to get around inside the 3D space. Next, we will actually implement sound into the demo provided. So turn the page, audio adventurer, and prepare yourself for the next level!

The Interactive Quiz for this Level is available in the App. In the Classroom, click on the Quiz book to test your knowledge!

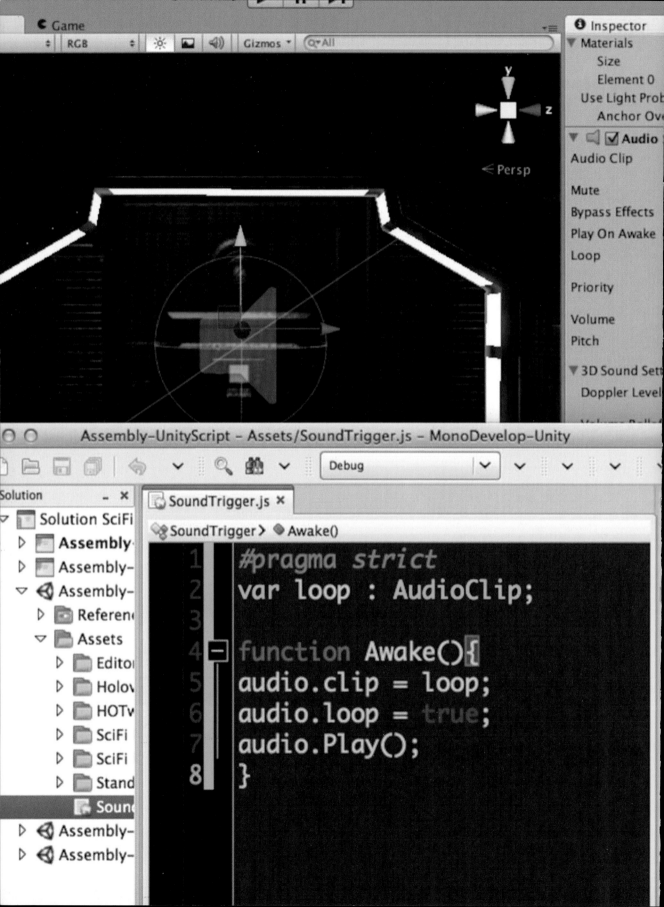

Game

RGB | Gizmos | Q▾ All

y
z
≼ Persp

Inspector

▼ Materials
  Size
  Element 0
  Use Light Prob
  Anchor Ov

▼ ◁ ☑ Audio
Audio Clip

Mute
Bypass Effects
Play On Awake
Loop

Priority

Volume

Pitch

▼ 3D Sound Sett
  Doppler Level

Assembly-UnityScript – Assets/SoundTrigger.js – MonoDevelop-Unity

Debug

Solution – ✕

▽ 🖥 Solution SciFi
  ▷ 📦 Assembly-
  ▷ 📦 Assembly-
  ▽ ◁ Assembly-
    ▷ 📁 Referen
    ▽ 📁 Assets
      ▷ 📁 Editor
      ▷ 📁 Holov
      ▷ 📁 HOTv
      ▷ 📁 SciFi
      ▷ 📁 SciFi
      ▷ 📁 Stand
         📄 Soun
  ▷ ◁ Assembly-
  ▷ ◁ Assembly-

SoundTrigger.js ✕

SoundTrigger ▸ ● Awake()

```
1  #pragma strict
2  var loop : AudioClip;
3
4  function Awake(){
5  audio.clip = loop;
6  audio.loop = true;
7  audio.Play();
8  }
```

Unity Too
Basic Audio Implementation in Unity 3D

Learning Outcomes:
Recognize settings when importing audio clips ·
Know how to trigger basic sounds in Unity ·
Understand the 3D settings of an audio source ·

Importing Audio into Unity

Audio Implementation

We've covered the basics of how Audio operates in Unity, the basic overall project structure and how to get around inside the game. We'll continue now with how to actually implement audio in a game environment, as well covering a few more advanced sound triggering options for those interested in what's available currently within the scripting API. This Level is going to involve scripting, and while you may not be doing this as a career, it's very helpful to know the basics of how triggering audio works. It's okay if you don't understand this the first time—scripting and coding are difficult things to grasp. Rest assured that there is enough general information in this chapter so that even

175

Go to the main classroom in the App, and click on the Videos screen to watch the step-by-step tutorials for this level covering how to implement and configure audio in Unity.

if you can't code like an expert, you can at least sound like one in a conversation.

Note: If you want to follow along with the step-by-step instruction below, you will need to have already downloaded Unity and our simple example project covered in Level 11.

Importing Sound

To take our next step, let's import some sounds. Find any sound file you have around and just drop it directly into the Project View. You'll notice it becomes a file that can be viewed and previewed. Click on it and let's cover a few of the options available when importing sounds into Unity.

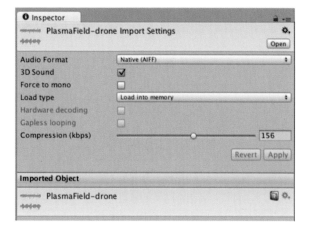

The first thing you should notice when you click on any audio file is the Inspector View fills up to show the Importing options. Unity refers to any audio file imported as an AudioClip. Let's take a look at the different audio importing and configuring options available to us.

NATIVE VS COMPRESSED MODES

Native Mode in Unity means that Unity will not touch the format of the audio file (uncompressed or not) and simply play it back as it was imported. Native Mode is usually recommended for short uncompressed audio sounds. **Compressed Mode** by contrast will compress the audio assets either as Ogg (Desktop) or MP3 (Mobile) when the project is compiled into an application. Note that Unity will not care if the files are already compressed when you import them—if you select Compressed Mode it will re-compress the audio again, which is usually undesirable and will likely create more artifacts.

COMPRESSED AUDIO LOADING MODES

These loading options are available when selecting the Compressed Mode:

- **Decompress On Load**: Unity will the decompress file when loading it. This is recommended only for shorter compressed files, as longer ones will potentially create a processing delay.
- **Compressed In Memory**: Unity will keep these files compressed until playback when they will be decompressed. Recommended for larger compressed files.
- **Stream From Disc**: This method is mainly desired for continuous sounds like music soundtracks. It uses lower amounts of memory but it's usually a good idea to limit the number of items that are continually streaming to one or two items.

OTHER IMPORT SETTINGS

- **3D vs 2D Sound**: This option is probably one of the most important overall. By default Unity will treat every newly imported file as a 3D AudioClip. This means that it will be heard through an Audio Source as if it's in the game space, which means that distance and position in relation to the Audio Listener will be taken into account. Most in-game sounds you will want to be 3D. Selecting the 2D option means the sound will not be affected by distance. This will be most useful for general ambient sounds or more commonly, your music soundtrack or interface sounds.
- **Convert to Mono**: this option will take any stereo file and convert it to mono, which can be desirable sometimes, especially in 3D contexts where stereo separation may be largely undetectable.

It's extremely important to point out in this Import window that after any change you make to the settings here, you must click **Apply**. This is a somewhat rare occurrence within the Editor, so it bears mentioning. If you forget Unity will remind you, just in case.

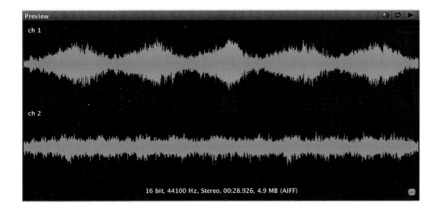

16 bit, 44100 Hz, Stereo, 00:28.926, 4.9 MB (AIFF)

Take a look in the inspector down below at the Preview area. This is where you can audition your sound file. You can play and stop your sound file (including playing from different locations by clicking on the

Pro Tip

While editing audio files destructively within Unity isn't possible, you can right click on any AudioClip in the Project and select **Show In Finder**. From here, you can open your audio file in the editor of your choice and save the changes. If you're planning on making a copy of any audio file and you want it recognized in Unity, it's definitely advised to save your copy outside of the Unity Asset folder and then bring it in via the drag-and-drop method.

waveform), you can toggle looping On or Off, and you can turn auto previewing On or Off. With this setting Unity will automatically play every AudioClip that's selected in the Project View. Notice you can't edit anything either—it's strictly bare bones here. Nonetheless it's definitely useful if you want to know if your sound loops properly in the game.

Putting a Sound into Gamespace

Selecting Objects to Add Audio Sources to

We already have an **Audio Listener** in the Scene (it's usually found as an included **Component** attached on the **Main Camera Object**. In this case it's attached to the object named **Player**). Now we need to add an Audio Source to complete the picture.

Select the **PlasmaField** object from the **Hierarchy**, or the **Scene View** (it's the large transparent colorful cylinder object), and press F with your cursor in the View. You should now be focused on the object.

We're going to add an Audio Source to this object so to do that we'll go to the Components menu and select **Audio**, and then **Audio Source**. Let's go over the basic controls:

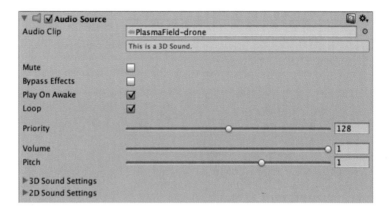

Audio Source Component Settings

The name of the Audio Source Component is at the top. Clicking on the name will minimize that part of the view. There's a check mark before the name. Use this check mark to deactivate or activate the Component. Activating and deactivating Components can be useful in troubleshooting.

The basic Audio Source settings are directly below the name, in the area above the colored graphic display indicating 3D Sound Settings. Note that by default, the AudioClip setting says None (AudioClip). You can change this by dragging the desired AudioClip directly over the None label and dropping it. You can also click the dot just to the right of this field to select the sound you want from the files listed there. Pick the file marked **PlasmaFieldDrone.aif** or select an ambient loop of your own choosing. When you do this, the **None** setting will change to the name of the AudioClip.

Notice that the settings state that this is a 3D sound. If you have deselected the 3D option for the sound file in the Inspector (remember, not the Audio Source—3D and 2D is file dependent), the settings will state that this is a 2D sound.

Let's go over the rest of the controls available:

- **Mute** temporarily mutes the sound. Mute can be useful when you need to isolate a particular sound from others. Leave this setting alone.
- **Bypass Effects** temporarily shuts off all effects that have been applied to the sound such as reverberation or other filters (most of these effects are available only in Unity Pro). Leave this setting alone as well.
- **Play On Awake** immediately plays the sound as soon as the scene is loaded. This setting is useful for ambient sounds. Turn this option on.
- **Loop** will loop the sound in the game. Note that checking this setting is different from using the Loop option in the Preview area, though it has the same effect. The Loop setting causes the Audio Source to loop continuously, so it is useful for background sounds. Turn this option on.
- **Priority** allows you to rank sounds according to their importance. When there are many Audio Sources, some may be less important than others and not need to be heard. You can rank sounds from 0 to 256: 0 indicates the most important sounds and is reserved for music soundtracks and other audio that must be heard, while 256 indicates a sound that does not need to be heard much at all. Leave this alone for now.
- **Volume** is the maximum volume the Audio Source will have: 1 is the highest volume possible, and 0 mutes the sound.
- **Pitch** is like a record speed control. Effectively, it adjusts the playback speed of a sound. Because speed and pitch are linked, a faster speed (above 1.0) creates a higher pitch with a shorter length, while a lower number (below 1.0) creates a lower pitch with a longer length. As we mentioned earlier in the book, this parameter can be immensely useful in creating an organic quality for several similar sounding sound effects.

3D Sound Settings

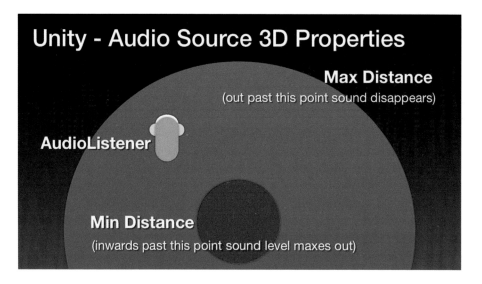

Unity uses the Min and Max Distances concepts in order to determine how sound is perceived within the 3D game space. These concepts are directly inherited from FMODs functionality. To think about how this works in an analogy, imagine two spheres placed one inside the other—you have an inner sphere and an outer sphere. The inner sphere represents the minimum distance that you are from the sound while the outer sphere represents the maximum distance. Note also that the number settings of Minimum and Maximum distance are expressed in GU or Game Units. This measurement is mainly metric in nature, so you can think of the settings in meters rather than feet, which is an important distinction to consider.

The **Min Distance** is the distance at which the sound will be at its maximum volume, and no matter how much closer you would be able to get to the Audio Source, the sound will not get any louder. Essentially it's the maximum volume that can possibly be obtained from the source as perceived by the Listener.

The **Max Distance** is the distance at which the sound will be perceived at all. Outside of the maximum distance of any Audio Source, the sound is silent. As you come closer to the Audio Source, the volume will gradually increase.

The difference in volume between the minimum and maximum distance of an Audio Source is governed by the rolloff curve, available in the 3D controls section. Let's take a look at this.

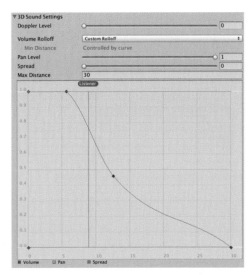

The 3D Settings shown here indicate a custom Rolloff. Note that the Min distance is now controlled by the curve.

The curve of the graph essentially governs the way that the volume will be reduced between the Min and Max Distance from an Audio Source. There are two preset modes—**Linear** mode, and **Logarithmic** mode. Although Logarithmic mode is considered more realistic to the way the human ear hears sound, Linear mode may be preferred in some cases, as the volume will drop off more gradually in comparison. You can also customize the curve by adjusting any of the nodes, or double-clicking the mouse to create more nodes. When you do so the menu will indicate that you are now creating/editing a Custom curve, and the Min Distance setting will blank out, because it is to be controlled by your custom curve rather than a preset distance.

In this case we've started with a Linear setting and then we adjusted it by adding a point to curve the line just slightly. We've set the Max Distance to 30, which will help to keep the sound localized.

There are a few more of these 3D settings to mention. Most of these can also be controlled by curves drawn in the same graph area as Volume:

- **Doppler Level**: This is a static control (no curve available) that changes the pitch of a sound based on the velocity (speed) of the Listener or the Source, enabling you to get semi-realistic effects when moving fast. It's not very convincing, however, as it only changes pitch and not phase. Best to use it sparingly or not at all.
- **Pan**: The pan control does not behave the same as a standard pan control in a typical stereo configuration. In effect, it governs how well

the stereo sound is perceived from the Audio Source within the 3D Game space. High settings will result in the stereo channel separation clearly being perceived, while low settings will tend to create more of a monaural sound, although still distributed through the 3D audio engine and 'heard' through the Listener.

- **Spread**: The spread control is most useful for surround configurations such as 5.1 or 7.1 surround systems. It governs how effectively the separation of individual speakers will be perceived inside the game from that Audio Source. Low settings will tend to make it sound more centralized and toward the front, while higher settings will distribute the sound more equally between all the speakers.

Let's now play our Scene so that we can hear the sound that we just put in our Audio Source. First, make sure that you save your Scene—this is going to be very important going forward. Then click the Play button at the top to play our Scene and listen to the looped AudioClip we placed in the scene as we walk around.

You'll recall the rule we specified last level that all changes to a Game Object in the Scene during Play Mode are lost. Actually here's where we should mention one significant exception of sorts, specific to Audio Sources that are set to both Loop and Play On Awake. First, make sure you're not playing your Scene. Then look at the Scene View bar at the top. You might have noticed a little speaker icon on the top bar towards the left.

Screenshot of audition mode icon.

Turning this on will automatically enable you to preview these Audio Sources in the game itself, although you'll have to move your view camera around to hear the effect of it. This can be a useful feature as you can then set and edit your Min and Max Distances and try things out before going into Game mode.

Triggering a Sound in Unity

Now, for our next trick, we're going to make it so that the character walking around will run into a door, and that will trigger a sound. You might recall in the last level, we talked about the importance of physics inside a game engine. That's what I'm going to use in order to generate this sound. Game objects inside Unity can have a Component known as a **Collider** attached to them. In fact for most simple objects that can be created by the Game Object menu this Component is already automatically added to them.

Let's take a look at the **Door** object. Search for this object in the Hierarchy, and click on it to review the inspector view for it. Look for the Box Collider component attached to the object. Now, find the **Is Trigger** option and click on it to enable the trigger functionality.

Add an Audio Source to this via **Add Component** Button>**Audio**>**Audio Source**.

In the Audio Source leave the **AudioClip** field blank and turn off **Play On Awake** and **Loop** if they're not already off. You might wonder how we're going to hear a sound now, since the Clip field is blank. The answer is that an Audio Source can just be a source of audio for a group of AudioClips. In fact you could trigger dozens of AudioClips to play through a single Audio Source. The significant limitation here is that it cannot adjust volume independently for all those files playing through them.

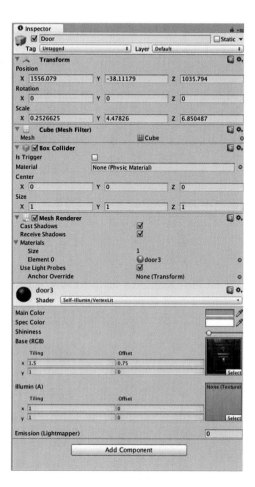

Setting Up A Script

OK, we have now reached the end of what's possible inside Unity without having to learn some code to go further. Fortunately it's not really hard to do these next steps.

1. Create a script in the Project View by clicking and holding the Create button and selecting Javascript.

2. You should then see this:

You need a better name than *NewBehaviourScript*. Highlight the script, and press Enter or click twice slowly.

3. Rename the script SoundTrigger (or any name you want—it does not matter). Ignore the warnings, if any.

4. Now you need to edit the script. Select the Sound Trigger script from the Project View and look at the Inspector View. In the upper left of the Inspector, click on the Edit button to open **MonoDevelop**, the default text editor in Unity.

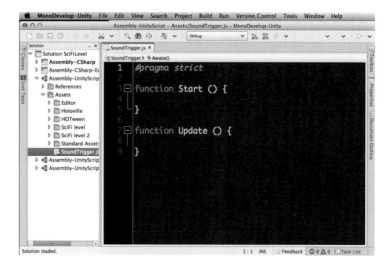

This is a fully fledged IDE (like we discussed earlier) that is set up for a type of Javascript (called Unityscript), Boo (a variant of Python) and native C# (more commonly associated with Microsoft Visual Studio). (Note: For any web coders out there, Unityscript is not the same as standard Javascript, but it's similar enough.)

5. Once it opens, delete whatever bit of script that already exists there. We won't need it.

6. Then type the following code exactly:

var Sound : AudioClip;

function OnTriggerEnter(){

audio.PlayOneShot(Sound);

}

So, let's analyze what we've just typed within the context of understanding the logic underlying the code:

Analyzing the Trigger Script

Line 1:

var Sound : AudioClip;

We begin by defining a variable known as **Sound**. The colon after "**Sound**" can be read as "is a type of". So this essentially means "define a variable called Sound that is a type of AudioClip". Notice that we end the line with a semicolon. This is extremely common practice in a number of programming languages.

Line 2:

function OnTriggerEnter(){

The function **OnTriggerEnter()** is an existing function that is associated with Collision events. A Collision event occurs when two objects with Colliders touch each other. In this case, the Collision occurs when anything encounters the Door. The Trigger is a special event of a Collider that is easier for the system to process. It also means that the objects will actually pass through each other rather than simply bump into each other.

Note the opening curly brace and the closing curly brace after the next line. This is the conventional part of the code that says, "If an object enters the trigger, then do whatever is within the curly braces."

Line 3:

audio.PlayOneShot(Sound);

Here's where the sound plays! The **audio.PlayOneShot(Sound)** command will play an audio file one time completely. What sound will it play? It will play the Sound variable we created on Line 1. You can specify which AudioClip in the code, but we'll do it an easier way.

Line 4:

Don't forget to close the curly braces to end the function:

}

Save this function in MonoDevelop by going to File > Save or by using the keyboard shortcut Command+S/Ctrl+S. Then close the editor. The text for the function should appear in the Inspector View and the script will be compiled. Any errors found in the script will appear in red at the bottom of the window or in the Console.

Apply the Script to the Intended Object

Now that we have a script done, what we can do is drag the script over the object that we want to use it on in the Hierarchy. First, find your script, and drag it over the Door object in the Hierarchy.

Look at the Door object in the inspector. Notice that it now has a Component with the name of the script that you just created added to it. You should also notice that there is a variable called **Sound** indicated on the script which should show "**None (AudioClip)**".

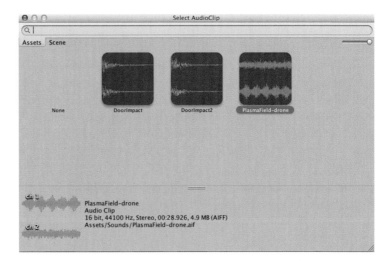

Click the small round button to the right edge to browse for **ImpactDoor. wav** or choose your own sound. You can also simply drag any audio clip from the project over this area, but be careful not to release the mouse button inside the Project View, or the Inspector View will change.

If you've done all of the above, you're finished! Now go reward yourself by starting up Game Mode and playing your Scene. Move your character into the Door and you should definitely hear a satisfying sound effect.

Help! I Can't Trigger the Sound

If you experience errors in compiling or anything else, ask yourself the following questions:

1. **Is your code completely accurate?** It has to be exactly as detailed earlier. If it's missing one character, such as a curly bracket, it can fail compilation and you won't be able to run your Scene.

2. **Did you drag an AudioClip to the script variable?** In this case you don't want to drag an AudioClip to the heading in the Audio Source Component because the method **PlayOneShot** requires a variable. So make sure you drag it instead over the Sound variable in the Script Component, not the Audio Source.

Trigger Dilemmas

So one thing that you might notice is that any object that you turn into a trigger automatically becomes transparent to whatever objects are passing through. This may not be the most desirable situation—for example, if you were to run into a Door you would not want to necessarily pass through the Door in order for the sound to play, but rather to literally collide with it. How would you do that? There are a lot of options at your disposal—coming strictly from a position involving only triggers, what you would do would be to create another object just in front but make it invisible. That way when you encounter the invisible trigger the sound will play and then you can take the trigger option on the Door object off, so that it behaves more like a real door would.

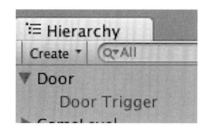

Fortunately a lot of this work is already done for you. Notice that the game object **Door** has a triangle next to it. Click the triangle to expose the object underneath it. It's called **Door Trigger**, and as you can see it's currently grayed out. This is because the game object has been deactivated. To activate and deactivate a game object click on it in the

Hierarchy and look in the upper left corner of the Inspector View. You should see a blank checkbox. Click the checkbox to activate the object.

You'll also notice that this new object is indented and underneath our original Door object in the Hierarchy. In Unity's terms, this object is referred to as a **Child**, while the object above it is referred to as a **Parent**. This is the method by which game objects can be organized in the Hierarchy, rather than files and folders in the Project View. In general children inherit behaviors from parents, but children can also be independent of parents if desired.

To see an example of this, click on the Door object, press the **W** key to change to the Translate Tool and then click on the colored arrows to move the object. You'll notice that when you move the Door object, its child (Door Trigger) will move along with it. However, you can also click on the child and move it independently of the Door object if you desire.

Let's return to the Scene. In the Door object, turn off its Is Trigger function in the Box Collider. This will make it into a solid object. To be safe you should also Remove your trigger script and Audio Source component by clicking on the Gear icon in the upper right-hand corner of the component and selecting **Remove Component**.

Now what we want is for the Door Trigger object to act like a trigger but not be visible. How do we do this? In this case, what we want to do is to turn off rendering for this particular object so that it remains active but invisible. To do this, find the Door Trigger object and look for the Component called the **Mesh Renderer**. Deactivate that Component by clicking the check box in the upper left-hand corner.

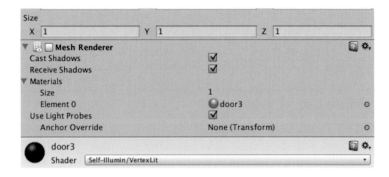

This makes the game engine not draw the object in question, but its functionality is left intact. Add the trigger script that you created in the earlier steps to the Door Trigger object instead. You'll also have to add an

Audio Source Component as well to complete the setup. Now, start up Game Mode and try it out. You will be able to run into the Door and not pass through it, but the collision sound will still be able to play.

Under the Hood: More Advanced Audio Triggering Methods

The following examples are for more advanced and code-savvy individuals wishing to know more specifically about the various ways that Unity can trigger audio. This is not for beginners, but it gives a more detailed look at the functioning of Unity's API and may be useful when explaining what you want to have happen to a programmer or integrator.

More Methods of Triggering Audio and Scripting Terms in Unity

There are a number of methods to trigger audio in Unity, and some are more useful for certain purposes than others are. Since version 4, a number of methods have been added that are not as well documented. We'll try to give a basic description of the usage cases as well as test examples to try out. Note that all of these methods will work with both Free and Pro versions:

First, a keyword is important: = audio here refers to a local Audio Source. If the script is placed on a Game Object with an Audio Source, audio specifically refers to that Audio Source. To refer to a specific Audio Source you can do the following:

This means set up the variable "myAudioSource" as a type of Audio Source:

var myAudioSource : AudioSource;

Play the sound (with optional delay time in parentheses (obsolete)):

myAudioSource.Play();

Any Audio Source must exist as a Component attached to a Game Object, so defining this variable means you would either drop the Game Object with the Source you wanted on it, or specify exactly which Game Object you want to use the Audio Source on. For now, we'll proceed locally.

audio.Play(<optional delay time>);

The simplest playback method, and the code equivalent to any Audio Source triggering an AudioClip, as we showed with the ambience loop example earlier. audio.Play() will play whatever audio clip has been selected, either by dropping it directly on the Audio Source Component, or specifying it in code with audio.Clip, as in the following:

```
var sound;
audio.Clip = sound;
loop = true;
audio.Play();
```

Use audio.Play(); for continuous sounds like music or background ambiences. It isn't generally good at retriggering sound effects. If Play() is invoked repeatedly on an Audio Source, the sound will interrupt and restart from the beginning. This method is also best for sounds that are moving in the space, or that you need continuous pitch or volume change on. Additionally an audio.Pause() and audio.Stop() command are available.

audio.PlayOneShot(<audioClip>);

This method is preferred for any layered sound effects you wish to create. Essentially what happens each time this method is called is that an individual unseen Audio Source is created, plays the sound, and is destroyed. PlayOneShot is great for when you want multiple copies, or instances, of a sound to exist. It is also important to know that while you can change the pitch or volume of a sound before triggering, it cannot be changed during playback.

audio.PlayClipAtPoint(<clip: AudioClip, position: Vector3>,initial volume: volume)

This method is somewhat similar to audio.PlayOneShot but will create an Audio Source and play the AudioClip at a specified physical location in the game represented by the Vector3 value. This is actually three numbers—for X,Y and Z locations). After playing it will clean itself up by destroying the Audio Source afterwards.

Note the differences here—PlayOneShot requires an Audio Source to be present but PlayClipAtPoint does not. This method also fixes a sound at the location specified (it can't move) and you cannot loop or change pitch of the sound before or after. You can set the volume in this method, or leave it out if desired. This method is great for something like a basic explosion sound to go along with a Prefab animation. The animation plays at the same time as the sound effect does, and the Audio Source is destroyed when it finishes playing.

Example

any Game Object can be dragged over the Transform variable. It will use that object's location at that point. For example, this will play the clip specified at the location at volume 0.9

var someLocation : Transform;

var mySound : AudioClip;

audio.PlayClipAtPoint(mySound, someLocation),0.9);

audio.PlayScheduled(<AudioSettings.dspTime : double>)

This is a new method that allows better much scheduling of an AudioClip, in combination with a separate absolute sample time called AudioSettings.dspTime, expressed as a **double** (double precision number—basically a very precise number).

This is much more accurate than the older method which is attached to frame rate. This rate can fluctuate depending on a number of factors, which can easily throw the music timing off. This method is independent of that timing and similar to the way that Wwise and FMOD Studio work. It works similar to audio.Play in that it needs an Audio Source and a AudioClip specified.

Example

Play a sound exactly 10 seconds later in the game:

var time = AudioSettings.dspTime;

var clip : AudioClip;

clip = audio.Clip;
audio.PlayScheduled(time + 10.0);

There is a lot more material on various ways to trigger audio in Unity, but as this is not a programming or scripting course we can't get into any more specifics here. This is as far as we're going to go for now.

Getting (More) Help

Now that we've just barely covered the basics of audio implementation in Unity, it does leave us with the question of "Where do I learn more about Unity?"

If you should decide to learn more about how Unity works in the broader sense or want to start making a game, there are a plethora, a smorgasbord, a dizzying array, a boatload—superlatives fail me—of documentations, tutorials, and videos available. There are four main sources of Unity knowledge referenced on their own website, under the Learn link:

Tutorials

A new section on the site is the increasingly comprehensive Learn section, with tutorial videos and demo projects to download on subjects like Audio, Editor, Scripting and more.

Documentation

This area consists of the **Manual**, **Component Reference Manual** and **Scripting Reference Manual**. These are all useful, but I find I refer to the Scripting Reference more often, as it has code examples I think are very helpful. These can also be accessed from the **Help** menu.

Community

This area consists of the Forum, the Unity Answers section, and Feedback section. Of these, the most useful for new developers is the Answers section, where coders from newbies to veterans pose questions that are answered by other members. The Forum and Feedback areas will become useful over time for connecting with other developers and for posting your availability as a composer or sound designer there.

Still not enough? Google "Unity 3D YouTube" and just see how many hits you get. There are literally hundreds of videos out there. Also, check the back of the book for all of our helpful links and publications or visit our Game Audio Resources page at the Game Audio Institute website for more info.

Unity Free vs Pro

The free version is non-crippled and completely functional in terms of scripting and publishing, supporting Mac/PC/Linux, iOS, Android, and Webplayer builds for no fee. However, there are a few significant tools and features that come with the Pro version which you should be aware of:

- **Dark Visual Theme**: Most obviously it supports an additional dark visual theme, good for working with projects in a low-contrast setting.
- **Profiling**: Being able to analyze the performance of the engine in various ways (including the sound triggering) is very vital. Unity Pro features robust profiling capabilities to help you tweak the performance of your App.
- **Audio**: All of the FMOD-derived effects like filtering, chorusing, delay, distortion, are only available in the Pro version. This is an unfortunate limitation for audio folks on a budget. These are all referred to as Filters and they adapt the sound of an Audio Source much like an ordinary plug-in on a DAW works. Earlier we discussed the various 3D settings in an Audio Source. Notably, the Low Pass Filter can be used in conjunction with the Audio Source in order to provide occlusion or obstruction effects.

As with paid-for Pro versions, the basic Pro license for the Editor as at the printing of this book does NOT include the Pro iOS or Android development packages, but all the bells and whistles will run on Mac, PC, Linux, and web platforms.

If you're wondering why I'm not mentioning the different Xbox, Playstation and Wii licenses, it's because they are made with certified developers of these platforms and are usually several thousands of dollars at minimum.

Conclusion

We've now come to the end of our time in Unity. We've spent time learning about the specifics of importing audio and the various settings available on Audio Sources. We've also investigated the basics of simple interactivity via scripting in order to trigger sound events, which is a very common thing to do inside games, and we've even covered a few other methods by which sounds can be triggered more accurately. There's a ton more that you can cover yourself if you're curious by investigating some of the sources we've mentioned. At the next Level we'll be looking at the recent explosion in the mobile, casual and social game markets.

The Interactive Quiz for this Level is available in the App. In the Classroom, click on the Quiz book to test your knowledge!

Back To The Future
The World of Mobile and Web Games

Learning Outcomes:
Overall knowledge of the mobile and casual gaming markets •
Distinguish between the functionality of the iOS and Android operating systems •
Understand how audio functions on mobile platforms •

There and Back Again: The World of Mobile Games

You've been learning throughout this book that games come in all shapes and sizes. Although most folks seem to concentrate on the latest high-budget, AAA titles (and certainly these games seem to garner the most press), an entire world of gaming takes place online and on phones, tablets, and other mobile devices. There's a big, big world of online and mobile gaming out there, and at the moment, it's growing much faster than the AAA console-based world is. This level focuses on that world and its unique sound requirements.

THE MORE THINGS CHANGE THE MORE THEY STAY THE SAME . . .

Technology has been on a path of miniaturization since the 1960s, when the transistor took over the vacuum tube, and the 1970s, when the integrated circuit miniaturized the transistor. Since then, we have been on an upward trajectory of speed and a downward trajectory of size. A decade into the new millennium, you could buy a phone with more CPU power, greater graphic power, and a lower price tag than the fastest computer made in the 1990s, and this trend has only increased since then.

In combination with the increase in technological sophistication, the online world that blossomed with the advent of the World Wide Web has matured as well. Companies are fully invested in Web 2.0 technology, fueled increasingly by open source approaches. Browsing on a smartphone looks almost exactly like browsing on a desktop, except for the size of the screen. E-commerce is a given. Digital distribution not only of music, but also books, movies, television shows, and, yes, games, is a regular part of everyday life. In an instant, someone on a computer, phone, or tablet can download nearly any kind of digital entertainment. Now that access to mobile and casual web-based games is nearly universal, the market is expanding at a tremendous rate.

From the standpoint of a seasoned game composer or sound designer, however, the experience of creating assets for these new mobile and web-based mediums is a case of Deja vu. Let's take a game franchise like Sega's *Sonic the Hedgehog*. It first debuted in 1991 for the Sega Genesis, which featured a maximum of 8KB of dedicated audio playback RAM (that's 1/128th of 1MB!), reading from a cartridge that could store a maximum of 4MB for everything in the entire game. No digital audio playback was possible—you had to use the onboard FM chips (six voices) and sound generators (three square waves and one noise channel) in conjunction with MIDI for all music and sound effects. Can you say limitations?

Sonic games created for later hardware increased the number of voices available, adding the ability to play digital audio samples as well as FM synthesis. CD-ROM gave way to DVD-ROM, and by the time 2010's *Sonic The Hedgehog 4: Episode 1* was released for multiple platforms (Xbox 360 and PS3), the channel counts and quality were so high that the hardware was no longer the limiting factor anymore.

At almost the same time the console version was released, SEGA also released an iOS version. Now, If you were hired to create sound for this version of the game, you would all of a sudden come face-to-face with hardware limitations again. This means 32 simultaneous software sound channels, plus considerably less RAM and application space to store audio assets. The iOS version does not roll the clock back to 1988, but the hardware limitations lie somewhere in the range of the late 1990s. The Xbox 360 version of this game by contrast has over 256 software audio channels available!

This is not a brand new phenomenon—over the years, there's been a lot of back and forth between high-end and low-end systems, all at the same time. Nintendo's Game Boy (see sidebar) broke open a huge market of rabid game fans willing to sacrifice performance for portability, and game audio professionals had to adjust accordingly. The Sega Game Gear version of *Sonic* had to make do with three Square waves and a noise generator playing in less memory than the Genesis allowed! So with that being said, let's explore the latest chapter of going back to the future, and examine this new emerging market.

For this level, we're interested in games created for a new generation of hardware and software not solely dedicated to the task of gaming, such as the iPad, iPhone, Android tablets, and more.

MOBILE GAME STYLES AND FORMS
Casual Games

These games are usually meant to be played in a relatively short period of time. Users may play, sometimes several times a day, from nearly any kind of device: a smartphone, a tablet, or a laptop. These games are designed for mass appeal and generally not targeted towards dedicated game fanatics. Casual games can cover a huge swath of gameplay styles and genres, from the relatively relaxed *Flow Free* (Big Duck Games) to the twitchy and fast-paced *Temple Run* (Imangi Studios).

One of the first well-known casual games was a version of the classic *Snake* game played on Nokia cellphones in the late nineties. Users could easily play this while on their commute, or waiting in line.

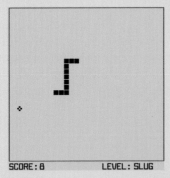

SCORE: 8   LEVEL: SLUG

A well-known blockbuster casual game is *Angry Birds* which catapulted (pun intended) its maker Rovio to instant stardom. The gameplay is utterly simple. A bird is used as ammunition for a slingshot, knocking down various structures in the process. The game involves fairly simple techniques, with levels that can be played quickly with satisfying results, as the blocks come tumbling down.

I Wanna Hold Your Hand

Handheld consoles were arguably the first mobile game platforms in existence and are still enjoying a fair amount of market share. Although there were devices used to play games as far back as the late 1970s, it was Nintendo's revolutionary Game Boy that firmly established the genre of portable gaming.

The Nintendo Game Boy

Designed in the early 1980s by Gunpei Yokoi, the same engineer who mentored Shigeru Miyamoto, the creator of *Donkey Kong*, the Game Boy arrived on the scene at exactly the right moment and with just enough power to play limited versions of Nintendo's popular arcade games. The unit featured two pulse wave generators, one PCM 4-bit wave sample channel, and one versatile noise generator. The unit only had one speaker, but headphones provided stereo sound.

Now, 30 years later, the Game Boy has also helped to inspire the whole chiptune movement. Modern day composers are using game technologies and retro sounds triggered directly from the audio card installed on the Game Boy itself bringing this classic sound to new audiences.

Chiptune artist Subatak is one of an increasing number of performers using Nintendo Game Boys to create live music. *Credit:* Medialab Prado.

After the Game Boy debuted, many rival console makers tried their hands at creating portable consoles. Some were successful, while others went the way of the dodo. Among all these various devices, two in particular stand out. The first is Nintendo's DS line of stylus-driven dual screen devices, debuting in 2004, and recently updated with the new Nintendo 2DS, and the second is Sony's PlayStation Portable or PSP line debuting in 2005, of which the newest member is the Playstation Vita.

Credit: Jeremy Engel.

As interesting as all these devices are, they don't exactly qualify as a mobile device per se, because essentially their sole purpose is to play games (though

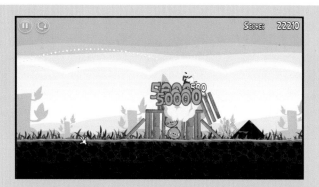

Although this category is changing rapidly, audio for these games will most likely be on the small side. You might be asked to create between 15–40 sound effects and 2–5 music loops. The number of lines of voice-over are greatly variable—some kids games may contain as many as 100 lines or more, while other titles might not have any.

Casual games are often single player-based games, but multiplayer games are very popular. Games such as *Words with Friends*, *Club Penguin* and *Monkey Quest* are good examples of the varied use of multiplayer environments.

There are also a few prominent variants in approach to casual games.

Adware/Spyware

The purpose of these types of games is to serve mainly as a promotional vehicle for the company that created them. The idea is that spending time on their site playing their game may create a favorable impression of the company as being cool or hip. Many of these games can also be spyware—that is software that tracks your behavior and preferences and sends that information to the company, for possible later marketing or potentially being sold to other companies.

Social Games

A social game's purpose is to serve as a gathering point for a number of players, all interacting within the game world in simple ways. Frequently, there are ways to interact with other players outside of the game to develop community. Quite often these games are

freemium—that is, free to play but with encouragements to spend more inside the game to level up or to clear obstacles faster. You can think of these as extremely stripped-down MMOs, with thousands or millions of players online at a given time.

Many of these games are based around social media sites like Facebook and Google+, as these provide an already established network of 'friends' you can play with, as well as a robust tracking infrastructure. Probably the best-known Social/Casual game is Zynga's *Farmville*, a game that is also an example of a freemium game. Gameplay is real-time and consists of constantly tending to your farm, while receiving or sometimes exchanging gifts to help with growing it.

devices like the PSP can certainly play movies and music just as easily). So we won't be focusing on these dedicated devices in any depth, except to say that limitations are also a fact of life for them. Even though each has its own set of unique restrictions and headaches, a lot of what's discussed in this Level can be directly applied to working on these platforms, should you have the opportunity to do so.

Sound design for these types of games is similar to a casual game with the added stipulation that a social game is often a work in progress, with assets being updated and added to on the fly. In the case of Facebook games the development is in Flash or HTML5, or even in Unity. Each of these come with their own audio issues, and your platform choices can limit you as well. Be prepared to create a variety of sound approaches depending on these various factors.

Operating Systems for Mobile Devices: iOS and Android

Realistically, we cannot cover every existing mobile platform because there are quite a few—including BlackBerry, Microsoft Windows Mobile, Motorola, PalmOS, and Symbian, just to name a few. Instead let's focus on two mobile operating systems that together account for well over half of the mobile operating-systems market—Apple's iOS and Google's Android.

Basics of Apple's iOS

The iOS platform was the first to set the standard as far as providing a viable and stable solution for game developers. Before iOS there was simply no single organized way to both purchase digital media and consume it in a high quality, seamless manner. Apple took advantage of the iTunes store-based culture they had established, along with the wildly successful iPod, to create a totally smooth experience for users, who flocked towards the new devices in droves. As a result, Apple's mobile iOS platform is still the choice of most game developers because of the simplicity and popularity of the App Store for consumers. Apple's App Store offers more than 900,000 iOS applications, which had been collectively downloaded more than 50 billion times as of June 2013, according to Apple at the Worldwide Developers Conference (WWDC). It has also paid out over $10 billion to developers, more than any other mobile platform combined.

STRUCTURE OF IOS

iOS is derived from the Mac OS X operating system. The foundation of these systems is Darwin, a UNIX-based core kernel and extension set that is present in every Apple computer. iOS contains four abstraction layers:

- The **Core OS** contains the Darwin kernel and vital system extensions.
- **Core Services** handles services such as in-App purchasing and XML support.
- The **Media Layer** contains media-oriented frameworks such as Core Audio and Core Display.
- **Cocoa Touch** contains the key frameworks for building iOS applications. This layer defines support for multitasking, touch-based input, and other high-level system services.

The latest version, iOS 7, uses approximately 2.5GB of a device's storage, although this use varies by device.

IOS AUDIO SPECIFICS

The iOS operating system uses a specially optimized version of Core Audio, the subsystem used on all Apple desktops and laptops. This system contains a lot of components and parts, only some of which you may use when implementing sounds for a game. It uses one hardware-accelerated channel that supports AAC (Advanced Audio Coding) and MP3 compression. The benefits of running audio in hardware on the iPhone or iPad are matters of priority and resources. It is best to trigger your most important sounds on this channel, so you don't have to worry about them not playing correctly and on time.

iOS also offers one software channel that supports up to 32 simultaneous streams, or tracks. These streams can play compressed audio, but software-based file decompression is more work for the CPU and thus may not play as fast or as reliably as audio triggered by the hardware channel.

Core Audio uses OpenAL, a low-latency positional (3D) audio architecture originally developed by Creative Labs, which provides Doppler and distance attenuation, but not occlusion or reverb.

This diagram shows the various services and libraries that make up Core Audio in iOS. In general, any application will use Core Audio as a go-between framework that addresses the device hardware and kernel drivers for audio. Any 3D positional effects or audio will be handled by a custom version of OpenAL.

iOS Sound Formats

iOS supports playback of many file types:

- **AIFF** (.aif, .aiff)
- **CAF** (.caf)
- **MPEG-1, layer 3** (.mp3)
- **MPEG-2** or **MPEG-4 ADTS** (.aac)
- **MPEG-4** (.m4a, .mp4)
- **WAV** (.wav)
- **MIDI** (.mid)

Linear PCM (uncompressed) audio or IMA ADPCM (IMA4) format (4:1 compression) are the suggested formats for playing multiple sounds simultaneously (or in close proximity to each other, such as for overlapping sounds) with iOS. In contrast, compressed formats such as MP3, AAC, and Apple's Lossless format can be played only one sound at a time, via hardware decoding. The standard iOS audio format is usually CAF, or Core Audio Format. CAF is a container, or wrapper format developed by Apple to hold just about any file type: AAC, AIF, WAV, ADPCM, and so forth. Apple developed CAF to offer a flexible container format that would work efficiently in all of their hardware products. Although it can be difficult to find an application that saves these file extensions, a few do support CAF file editing.

- **Pro Tools** imports CAF files but cannot export them.
- **Apple Logic Pro X** can import and export stereo and mono CAF files, but not multi-channel files.
- **Apple GarageBand** can import but not export CAF files.
- **Audiofile Engineering Sample Manager** can import and export uncompressed CAF files, but it is not an editor per se.
- **Audacity** can import and export uncompressed CAF files for editing.

As of version 4.2, iOS offers MIDI support, which includes communication with other devices over wired/wireless connections, as well as MIDI file playback. In addition, music-software developer SONiVOX has created a library of sounds that can be organized into SoundFont or DLS (DownLoadable Soundbank) sound banks.

Writing Games for iOS

iOS uses Objective-C for its basic code structure, which is handled by the Xcode integrated development environment (IDE). Xcode software comes free with every OS X Installer and can also be downloaded from Apple's website for free with a registration. Applications such as Unity also create builds of a game for iOS as an Xcode project, so the final touches can be added and the application built and compiled in Xcode.

Some provisioning applications allow the user to paste in the UDID. Recently, some services can also detect the UDID via a website connection, doing away with the need to copy the device ID from iTunes.

Google's Android

Hot on the heels of Apple's unveiling of the iPhone SDK, Google followed up with the first announcement of its new mobile operating system: Android. This operating system is a mostly open-source-based system centered around a Linux kernel, although the kernel has been heavily modified enough, so that it is now considered a fork, or separate version. In fact, at this point, full compatibility with existing Linux systems is quite difficult to implement. Similar to Apple, Google has been taking steps to make sure app and hardware developers don't fragment their codebase.

Credit: Jeremy Engel.

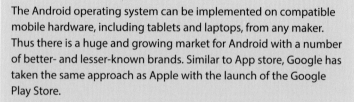

The Android operating system can be implemented on compatible mobile hardware, including tablets and laptops, from any maker. Thus there is a huge and growing market for Android with a number of better- and lesser-known brands. Similar to App store, Google has taken the same approach as Apple with the launch of the Google Play Store.

One difference between iOS and Android is that device makers supporting Android can implement certain features or applications voluntarily. As a result, Android's market is more atomized and varied. Depending on the device you use, certain features are available and others disabled. Still, the overall trend is that older, less-featured versions are becoming less common. Like iOS, Android has gone through several revisions. Each is named after a dessert: Cupcake, Donut, Eclair, Froyo, Gingerbread, Honeycomb, Ice Cream Sandwich, and Jellybean, with Kit Kat being the most recent.

SOUND ON ANDROID

Sound on Android is handled mainly by its Linux kernel, and requires OpenSL ES to run. This is an embedded device library that is roughly similar to OpenAL. One big difference is that OpenSL ES does include MIDI Support. OpenSL ES uses what it calls Profiles to help carry out basic audio tasks. These tasks include music playback (similar to iPod or other players), plus phone UI and ringtones. There is also a more full featured version of OpenSL ES that is used for gaming and features positional (3D) audio, effects and more.

Pro Tip: Latency

One thing that bears mentioning is that, at the present time, noticeable delays when triggering sound in Android are just a fact of life. Getting true low-latency audio in an Android game is pretty challenging. You have to deal with software and hardware specifications that can vary widely. This means that responsive audio that reacts to user input (like pressing a button, for example) can suffer from timing issues that are undesirable (this is especially true when having to decompress audio on the fly). This has led in some cases, to developers having to choose between triggering music or sound in their applications. Currently, there's not one magic bullet that will solve all these issues, but many engineers and experts are working to close the gap.

This diagram shows the use of Android hardware for game audio. Applications will use the MediaPlayer side of the structure usually. Any 3D positional effects or audio will be handled by a custom limited version of OpenSL ES. All audio data must then be mixed and decoded into PCM streams as an AudioTrack. The AudioFlinger is an audio server framework that then takes the audio data and routes it to the hardware via different kernel sound drivers (chiefly ALSA).

Most hardware running Android supports the playback of the following file types:

- AAC (.aac, .Mp4a)
- MP3 (.mp3)
- Ogg Vorbis (.ogg)
- FLAC (.flac)
- WAV (.wav)
- MIDI (.mid)

The inclusion of Ogg Vorbis in this list is significant. In addition to being entirely open sourced in terms of hardware and software (meaning it can run in an operating system or be encoded in a hardware chip), Ogg Vorbis is an increasingly common format for game audio. Interestingly FLAC is also included. This is a data-compression format that does not change the original audio data; it merely fits the data into the smallest space possible, usually achieving 2:1 compression. AIFF support does not seem to be natively included. Playback on Android is roughly similar to iOS—1 hardware mono or stereo PCM channel, and numerous software streams controlled by a mixer API. MIDI playback is made possible in Android through the embedded SONiVox Jet system.

GENERAL CONSIDERATIONS FOR WORKING ON MOBILE GAME PLATFORMS

Space

Space is probably the biggest consideration for games developed for mobile game platforms. Mobile devices are by design less powerful and offer fewer capabilities than desktops and laptops. They frequently have less RAM and smaller hard-disk space. Files need to be small, and compression should be used whenever possible. Mobile gamers rarely play games in situations in which high-quality sound can be distinguished from medium-quality sound. Often players on a phone or portable device are hearing sounds coming from very small speakers or substandard headphones.

Speed Kills

Speed is next in line and has a huge effect on how you deal with sound and the amount of available bandwidth. In some games, audio content is actually streamed over a network connection instead of being stored on the device. Internet connection bandwidth affects the speed at which all of the game data will travel, and this can vary greatly. Currently the most popular explosion in the market is with mobile devices rather than desktops and laptops. These devices may run over WiFi networks, or they can use their own dedicated network connections.

For bandwidth, 3G (third-generation) speeds, which are equivalent to low- to mid-level DSL speeds (3–6Mbps (mega-bits per second)), are considered low- to mid-speed connections, and companies are now providing LTE (long-term evolution) and 4G (fourth-generation) speeds nationwide. These speeds are usually in the range of 8–11Mbps, though theoretically, throughput of the specification goes up to 100Mbps.

Prepare for a Variety of Possibilities

The big takeaway from of all of this is that you have to be prepared for varying levels of performance when working with mobile games. Nobody likes to wait for audio assets to load for too long, even if they sound awesome. In some cases, producers may remove sounds if they cause too much of a downgrade in gameplay performance. Back in the days of dial-up modems (AKA the stone age) media could be found in low (dial-up) and high (DSL) bandwidth versions. In today's games, bandwidth is dynamic and generally shifts automatically between high and low quality, or in many cases, just shoots for the lowest common speed available. These dynamic shifts in speed and performance are something you have to be savvy to. You must be prepared to work with the development team on the overall loading and unloading of sound assets, so that your sounds don't disrupt gameplay, yet still get the attention they deserve.

Tips for Working on Mobile Game Platforms

Consider what corners you can cut to reduce file size. For example, do your sound effects really have to be at 16 bit, 44.1KHz? Sometimes a more limited frequency response will have no discernable effect on end sound quality, due to the type of sounds (simple, short duration impact sounds, for example) or the frequency response of the speaker it is being played on. In a case like this, downsampling to 16-bit, 22KHz might save you some space and maybe even increase performance! It's okay to have your voice-over, SFX and music at different sample rates, as long as the engine and operating system allow it.

Audio compression for ambient backgrounds is a given! Remember, 2 minutes of stereo audio uses over 20MB, which is a ton for a mobile game. By editing your ambient loops as efficiently as possible, and using a compression scheme like MP3 or Ogg Vorbis, you can save valuable space and keep the audio quality as high as possible. You might also reconsider using MP3 at high bit rates. It sounds great, but not all portable devices will support it. The same is true for variable bit rate files (these are files where the encoding rate can vary depending on the complexity of the music). To be safe, it's generally best to use constant and common bit rates.

If typical 10:1 compression via MP3 or Ogg isn't available at 128Kbps, try IMA ADPCM, an early audio-compression codec that works on a 4:1 compression ratio that cuts file size down to 25 percent of the original size. Though the result will be lossy compared to the original, it's a good compromise that preserves more of the original sound.

Don't assume that MP3 files will loop seamlessly. Did you know that MP3 encoding can wreak havoc on perfectly good looping files? It's sad but true . . . this is because the MP3 format allocates file space in blocks or frames. When there are not enough samples to fill an entire frame, blank space is inserted to fill the void. Engines like Flash and Unity deal with this problem internally but, when programmers try to call converted files directly from external databases, skipping is likely to occur. Know your platforms and make sure that you don't get blamed for sloppy implementation!

Mixing Your Audio for Small Format Delivery

Mixing for mobile requires creative thinking and problem-solving skills. Just like mixing audio for any other medium, it's always best to listen to your mixes on the device itself. In some cases, this might be either impossible or expensive. Small format games get played and listened to in lots of different environments, from city streets, to the back seats of automobiles. The challenges of creating a uniform audio experience are daunting and complete control may not be possible—a hard pill to swallow.

Mobile devices tend to have small speakers, some only as big as your thumbnail. As a result the accurate playback of bass frequencies can be one of the biggest issues. To make things even tougher, dedicated gamers looking for a more immersive experience might be wearing headphones, or routing the audio through Bluetooth to their stereo, where the bass will definitely be pumping. So how can you satisfy all of these situations?

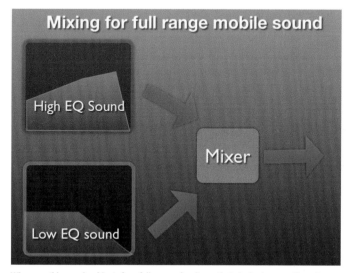

When possible you should mix for a full range of audio, so that playback on small speakers and in headphones or stereos is possible. Harmonics are going to be your friend in this situation. Avoid pure sine tones in the bass range unless you have an obvious complement in the higher range for small speakers.

One possible solution would be to design your sounds so that they contain a wider variety of harmonic information. Take the case of a death metal kick drum—the main kick's fundamental is around 80Hz, so there's no way a typical mobile speaker can hope to reproduce that. However there's also a beater sound around 2.5KHz and higher, and that's perfectly perceivable in this context. By including both sounds in your sample, you have now created a situation where small speaker playback will catch the upper frequencies and full range playback will also reveal the low end. This technique is also very effective for all kinds of sound effects, from explosions to clicks and rollovers. Think of it as getting two sounds for the price of one!

HTML5: The Pitfalls of a New Standard

A while back, Apple started a trend away from Adobe's ubiquitous Flash platform with its iPhone and iPad devices in favor of HTML5. In 2007, HTML5 was a highly regarded blip on the radar of Internet and web design standards, and not due out in full adoption and release until 2014. Apple's announcement gave it a huge push forward, and as a result HTML5 adoption has been on the rise ever since. The trouble was, and currently is, that there are no all-in-one solutions for developing interactive content that will run on every device using HTML5. Up until Apple's divesting of Flash support, a Flash game could run on nearly every hardware platform in existence, and still has an over 90 percent adoption rate online. The exclusion of Flash from the tablet and mobile markets has sent shockwaves through the development community. Keep in mind that the tablet market was small when Apple made its move, and touch-based interaction was revolutionary. Now, tablets are all the rage and the tools for simple content creation are just not ready for prime time.

HTML5 also comes with its own set of issues. One of these is the lack of web-browser standards support across both browsers and platforms. Currently, Apple's Safari, Mozilla Firefox, and Google Chrome offer the most HTML5 support, leaving out Microsoft's Internet Explorer (IE), although version 10 has closed the gap a certain amount and 11 is set to improve the score. Flash has been ubiquitous and quite easy to use, but has virtually no representation in the tablet market. HTML5 is on the rise, but the drawback is that, as of this writing, there isn't an equally functional HTML5-based App that has all the capabilities and ease of use that Flash does. This means that nearly all functionality within the element has to be coded by hand. To the extent that a developer was already doing most of the coding in ActionScript 3, Flash's well-known scripting language, the shift to HTML5 and JavaScript is not as big a deal, but to the more inexperienced and less code-savvy (including audio professionals), there aren't a lot of options.

Oddly enough, Adobe is addressing some of these issues with their Creative Cloud series of cloud-based services, somewhat similar to Google's but focused on graphic and media publishing. The tools, called Edge, are focused for web and mobile web developers. Before they stopped development, Adobe also updated Flash CS6 Professional to support output to JavaScript instead of SWF, using a series of tools called CreateJS, which has smoothed the path even further.

For audio professionals the current environment is just as challenging as the one for graphics professionals. Audio playback in HTML5 comes with its own <audio> tag and that tag provides some useful characteristics, like support for compressed audio formats (like Ogg Vorbis, for example). The actual functionality of that audio tag for use in video games is currently—well, "inconsistent" would be putting it nicely. As a result of this currently broken approach, a number of solutions are being proposed. Currently SoundJS and SoundManager 2 provide relatively decent functionality, using a combination of HTML5 audio and Flash fallback when HTML5 audio isn't supported.

ENTER THE WEB AUDIO API

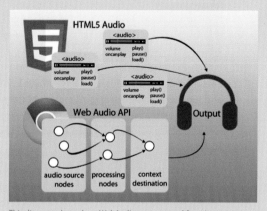

This diagram shows how WebAudio routes sound from its various input nodes to the output context, which can be thought of as a master output on a mixer.
Credit: Mike Pennisi from bocoup.com blog post.

The Web Audio API is one of the most robust solutions to have emerged and is poised to potentially become the dominant audio solution. The Web Audio API, when supported in a browser, allows the kind of functionality only dreamed about for current web audio. The Web Audio API supports extensive sample playback, including things like live filtering, reverb, binaural panning, and much, much more. Currently Web Audio API is supported in versions of Google's Chrome, Apple's Safari, and recently Mozilla's Firefox joined the fray, meaning that support of Web Audio is now around 65% of all browsers on desktop and mobile devices. Internet Explorer is still lagging far behind and the status of IE 11 is unknown at this time.

For a demonstration of the awesomeness of HTML5 audio using the Web Audio API, check out the following links (all of these require the Chrome browser to run):

Jam with Chrome: A Google Chrome Experiment
www.jamwithchrome.com

Pedalboard.js: Guitar Pedals in the Web Browser
http://dashersw.github.com/pedalboard.js/demo/

Flash Is Dead—Long Live Flash!

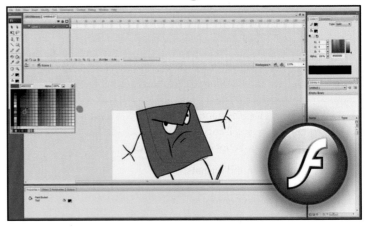

This revolutionary platform literally once ruled the roost of the casual games market, not to mention sites like YouTube, and millions of rich media content-oriented websites. Interestingly, it was deployment on mobile devices that proved to be Flash's Achilles heel. Although hardware like the Blackberry and Nokia phones, among many others, started to implement the mobile version of Flash, the results were far less than stellar. Stuck with the slowest data speed, UMTS or EDGE, Flash proved to be a huge battery drain on many devices, and often contained security holes that could be exploited.

It was Apple, though, and Steve Jobs in particular, with his penchant for killing obsolete features (like the floppy disk, and most recently the optical drive on Apple's MacBook Air), who summarily announced in 2010 that the iOS, as it came to be called, would never support Flash. This was much more than an idle threat—the iPhone and iOS, combined with the iTunes Store, was a runaway success and gave iOS a majority in market share of mobile operating systems. For mobile games it was a death knell, and Adobe conceded defeat in 2011, killing further development of Flash for browsers on mobile devices.

Although we have spent some time discussing the impending demise and replacement of Flash by HTML5 and JavaScript, don't count Flash out just yet. Remember, Flash can still run as a local application on the major mobile platforms like iOS and Android. There are also a huge number of browser-based Flash games still being played on Mac, PC, and Linux desktops. Facebook, one of the world's biggest social network sites, still uses Flash for its browser-based games.

Audio for Flash

Let's discuss the workings of Flash from a content-creation perspective. Audio usage in Flash is both simple and complex. On one level, it's easy to insert audio and understand its function in the Flash interface. On another level, it requires the hand of an integrator or a programmer to discern the best ways to call and integrate sound into a Flash game or application using ActionScript or JavaScript libraries.

Flash handles several sound formats:

- AAC (Advanced Audio Coding)
- AIFF (Audio Interchange File Format, for Mac only)
- MP3 (Moving Pictures Expert Group—Audio Layer 3)
- AVI (Audio Video Interleave)
- WAV (Waveform Audio format)
- Au (the audio format developed by Sun Microsystems)

NOTE: MIDI is not supported in FLASH

SOUNDS IN FLASH

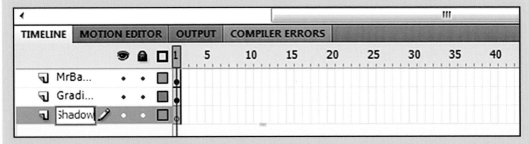

Flash provides a basic interface for performing simple audio functions. In Flash, sounds can be inserted into the Library of an existing project and placed on a timeline so the audio can be looped, volume balanced, faded in and out, and timed to particular screen events. Native audio-compression codecs then render out the audio with the rest of the project into a file format called SWF, short for Shockwave Flash. (Shockwave was a multimedia audio library created by Macromedia and subsequently folded into Flash.) SWF is a container format that holds all creative elements of a game or application created in Flash.

Sound can also be called from an external sound library. Sound triggered in this manner must already be fully mixed and compressed because the programmer simply points to the sounds and they are played back at the appropriate timing.

NOTE: Sound called from external MP3s can create the same skipping problem that we mentioned earlier due to the usage of frames rather than samples. Sounds imported into the Flash timeline, however, can be set to loop seamlessly.

Flex-Based Solution

Sound can be called in Flash in a third way, which avoids this problem. Although many programmers and developers new to Flash development tools are unaware of this solution, sounds can be imported into a standalone instance of Flash and batch-compressed using native MP3 compression within Flash. The entire library can then be exported as an SWF file. The programmer can then catalog that file and its contents, so it can be called into the game or program. The end result is audio that makes full use of the audio tools and native compression within Flash and still loops properly and seamlessly when it is called externally.

Conclusion

We've once again covered a lot of ground, and yet barely scratched the surface of audio for a new generation of gaming. As time progresses you will see which predictions we've made are accurate, and which others fall by the wayside. One thing you can count on, there are sure to emerge as yet unforeseen solutions to the mobile conundrum. Right now mobile gaming is still a bit like the Wild Wild West—maybe a bit more civilized in many places but still with a lot of pitfalls, rattlesnakes, and ambushes for the unwary audio traveler. Hopefully, with this guidebook under your belt, you'll be just a little bit more prepared. Next, we're going to talk all about you, and how you might be able to turn all this information into an actual career. The final level awaits, so read on!

The Interactive Quiz for this Level is available in the App. In the Classroom, click on the Quiz book to test your knowledge!

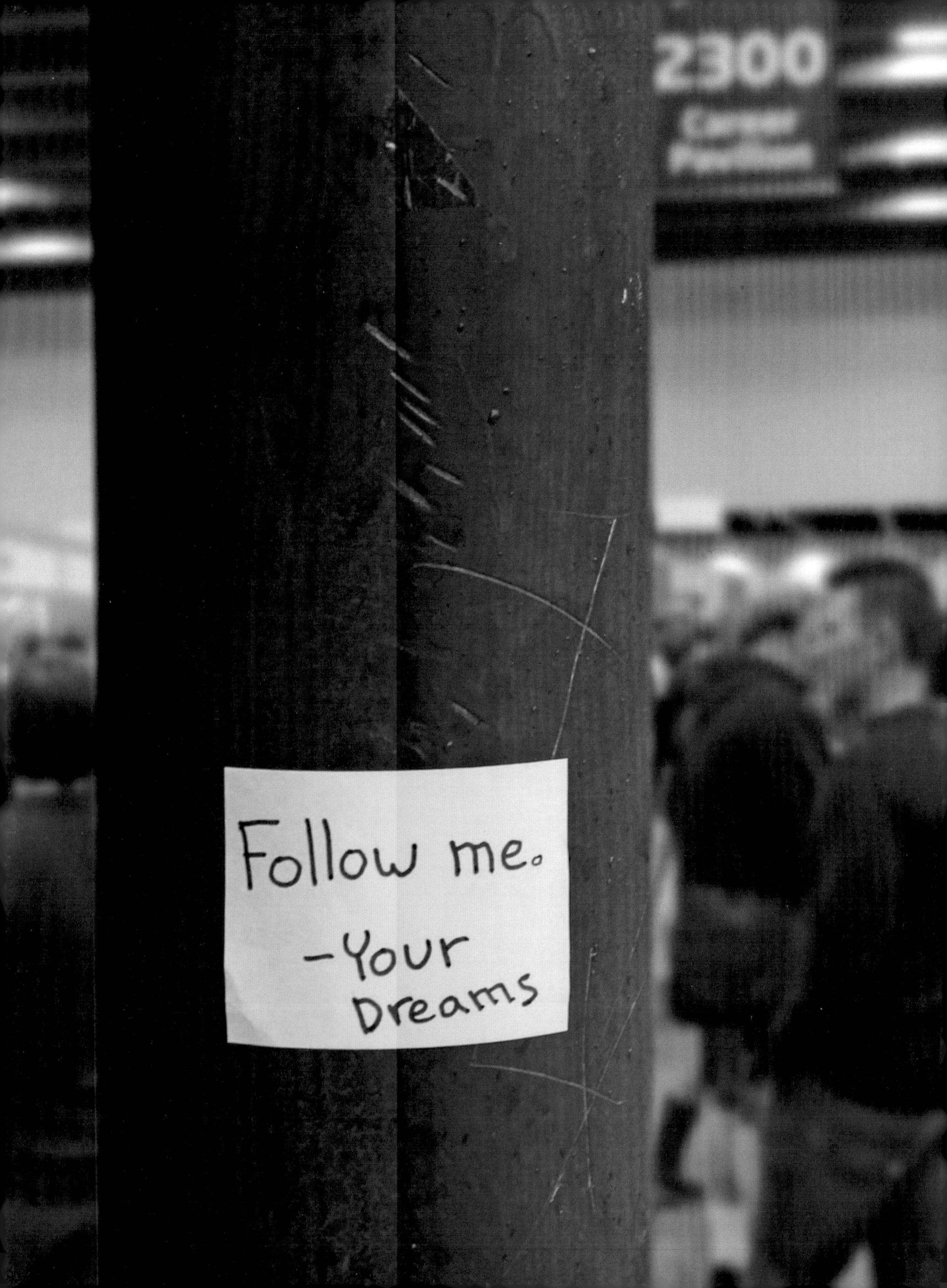
2300
Follow me.
-Your
Dreams

Show Me The Money
Getting a Job in Sound For Games

Learning Outcomes:
Identify careers opportunities in sound for games •
Know how to develop a media rich portfolio website •
Understand the business of game audio •

Getting Into the Game Audio Business

The business of games is huge. There's room out there for composers, players, producers, engineers, implementers and many more. Roles and titles change all the time, in previous levels we have gone through many of the most common roles that exist in the industry. Armed with this knowledge, you should have a general overview of who you might meet out in the field and a basic understanding of what they do.

Now it's time to think about what **you** want to do. What are your strengths and weaknesses and how can they be put to best use? This level is all about you—nice, right?

The first fact of life in business is adaptability. Games are a rapidly changing, fast-paced and high-tech industry. The more adaptable you are, the clearer your options will become.

JOBS IN SOUND: STEVE'S *GRAND THEORY OF ADAPTATION!*

Behold, *The Grand Theory of Adaptation*, a custom six-step program (who needs twelve?). Also known as "perseverance squared." You must have a focused goal, but also keep an open mind to the twists and changes in the road. View your art and the business of it in a broad scope. Let's get started . . .

1. Quality

Your work must be good. What do I mean by this? Well, since sound is such a subjective topic, nobody really knows what "good" means except you. What is important is that you make *your* sound (whatever that is) as good as it can be. I studied composition with Stephen "Lucky" Mosko, and he always talked about the morality of a piece of art. Remember, sound is a living thing, and your sounds want something from you. Don't be afraid to give 100 percent or more!

2. Perseverance

Don't be turned from your path. Keep plugging away, and doors will open. Follow your muse. Go ahead and quit your day job or, even better, don't get one in the first place if possible, or at least go part time. Do the work and expose yourself to a wide range of experiences. If it's better somewhere else in the world, go there—you just might dig it. In the United States, the game industry is quite active in the San Francisco Bay Area, Seattle, LA, and Austin, Texas. Other cities are developing, like New York and Boston, but these are currently the biggest markets. Internationally, Vancouver, London, Berlin, Munich, Amsterdam and Tokyo are all thriving markets for game development. Don't be afraid to follow the money!

3. Parallel Movement

Things don't just go up and down, they often go side to side. To get out of a windy harbor, a sailboat often has to use tacking, or a zig-zagging course. Back and forth, side to side—though it seems like you are going nowhere, and it might make you seasick, you'll get out sooner or later. Sometimes, time spent developing some other facets of your audio personality will lead you to places you never knew about. Being well-rounded is not a bad thing. If you are a composer, knowing a bit about implementation can't hurt. Or if you are a sound designer, playing or understanding music is a good thing.

4. Conceptual Continuity

This is massively important. If you're just getting started in this field, you'll want to try out a bunch of different things, such as composing or sound designing for a wide variety of genres. It's totally fine and even expected to wear a lot of hats in this industry. However, you need to listen to your muse at all times. Stay on your path by having conviction and working to your strengths. Your work needs to reflect your passion for it, and when you change it too much to satisfy others' desires you can lose your passion and your identity. Keep your compass by doing what's right for your heart and soul. It's easy to get side tracked while looking for work but it is important especially at the early stage of your career to try and figure out what speaks to you.

5. Tell the World

You must find a way to let folks know what you are up to. In this overcrowded day and age, press and publicity are a must. Social media, websites, tweeting and more are required. Let people frequently know what you are up to and what projects you are working on by keeping your networks updated.

6. Critical Mass

You do the same thing long enough, keep making stuff, and sooner or later you will reach a tipping point. The author Malcolm Gladwell in his book *Outliers* frequently refers to the 10,000 hour mark as a point for excellence, meaning that if you've done anything for that many hours you've essentially mastered that skill, and your work will reflect this mastery. There are so many examples of this. There are also a number of examples of geniuses that died poor and lonely despite that mastery. Well, you choose a career in the arts, and risk is part of the game.

Questions, Questions, Questions!

You need to spend time thinking about your ideal job in this narrow yet diverse realm. It's important that you try to find a job that you enjoy and are passionate about. Passionate workers create the highest quality work. Remember *The Lord of the Rings* film trilogy? Almost everyone on the set and in the crew was a huge fan of the books, so everyone involved was dedicated to making something worthwhile and beautiful. Costume designers spent hundreds of hours making elaborate designs that appeared on screen for only a few seconds—that's how passionate they were about the project. Start by asking yourself the following questions.

Go to the Classroom in the App, and click on the Video screen get more practical tips about the business of games!

Credit: Veronique Deboard.

Do you find yourself attracted to creating music or sound?

In most cases, I would hope the answer to this question is a resounding "Heck Yeah!!" Many of you may even be massively inspired by the amazing music soundtracks and sound design in such AAA game series as *Battlefield*, *Assassin's Creed*, *Bioshock*, *Dead Space*, *Mass Effect*, *Dragon Age*, and countless others. However, being a sound designer or composer for an AAA console game is equivalent in stature to being the sound designer or composer for a summer blockbuster movie. There unfortunately aren't that many positions available at the top. You can get there, with a lot of talent and dedication, but you'll probably have to work your way up over time.

However, there are many opportunities in the indie console game world. The huge influx of social and mobile games is another huge and expanding territory, and you can also gain experience while you are in school.

Here are some additional questions to ask that might help you direct your interests to one of these areas within the broader definition of game audio job positions.

Do you have programming experience or are you interested in programming or scripting in general?

Answering yes to these questions directs you toward the implementation or integration side of things. You might also find middleware such as FMOD or Wwise to be more to your liking. Bear in mind that the industry is sorely in need of capable implementers and especially programmers. Taking a look at programming languages: Javascript, Objective-C (for iOS games), and Java/C# for Android are just a few examples. Keep in mind that how deeply you get into the programming side is a personal choice. But, it's never a bad idea to have a general idea of how these things work.

Are you interested in the idea of music or sound that continually evolves within a game environment?

Answering yes to this question puts you firmly in the camp of adaptive music or sound. Although the market for specialists in this subfield is growing, adaptive music and sound is not always the most common approach to handling audio in a game environment, mainly because it can be complex to integrate. Nevertheless, if you are interested in this field, you should also study middleware because these tools are used extensively in adaptive audio for games. This developing field can also encompass new methods of generating sounds inside the games using various types of synthesis. Although it's difficult to predict what technologies will be used in the future, it's a fair bet that adaptive and generative audio in games will become easier and more powerful to implement.

Are you a good networker? Do you get inspiration by working with others?

Answering yes to these questions means you like working in groups, which is a great thing because game development is almost always a team sport. It may also mean that you are good at being a go-between or liaison. At the bottom end, these skills may make you an effective production assistant (PA) or gofer, which may not be your end goal, but at the top end, these same skills will make you an effective producer or audio director. Working well with others and being able to network is a great skill to have in any field.

Marketing Yourself: Preparing a Killer Resume, Portfolio and Website

Once you have determined what you like to do and what you are passionate about, the next step is to start marketing yourself and your services to interested parties. Marketing is incredibly important. In this challenging and competitive environment, jobs just don't fall off the trees. Companies won't come to you. You must beat the bushes, scour the Web, establish a network of contacts in the industry, and, above all, make yourself and your work look as good as possible. The chief way to do this is with a strong portfolio website.

DESIGNING YOUR WEBSITE

A good portfolio website is like a good resume. You should emphasize your strongest skills, focus on the types of experiences you have had within the field, demonstrate your familiarity with applications, and showcase your best work.

Create an audio-based website that shows audio and video clips chiefly. If you are a sound designer, include more than just individual sounds; also include games for which you designed the majority of sounds. If you are interested in composing, you should include examples of music in various styles. You have a few options for including this work.

Include gameplay clips. The easiest, most direct way is to upload a video clip that shows between 2 and 4 minutes of gameplay in action. You can also link to clips on YouTube or similar services.

Interactive is Best! Including Web Players

The best way to showcase your work as a game audio professional is to include interactive real time gameplay examples. This can be tricky and requires a bit more technical implementation, but a web player game on your website allows interested employers to experience gameplay firsthand in the browser environment. It's a more ideal method of showcasing interactive/adaptive sound design or music for games and is generally a much better showcase for your skills in Interactive media.

As we've discussed, Unity offers the ability to build out your project as a WebPlayer build, which can play in a browser. Bear in mind that doing this requires that the viewer downloads a plug-in that is not standard with most web browsers, so your website should include a prominent link to obtain the plug-in. Also keep in mind, mobile devices cannot currently display WebPlayer builds. The best method is probably a combination of these two options, so prospective employers can easily watch videos of gameplay or download the plug-in to play the game in the browser themselves on a desktop PC or Mac.

Again, you should provide a variety of individual sounds to show your creativity and versatility in creating sounds for different purposes. It is also a good idea to use a Flash or JavaScript/HTML5 player to organize your clips (Javascript/HTML5 are preferred over Flash, especially for iOS users).

Soundcloud Audio Players/Playlists

In addition to playthrough movies or web players, a Soundcloud account is a very common way to showcase your work. Soundcloud is free for under 2 hours of audio (120 minutes) and features many embedded players (including HTML5-based ones) that you can incorporate into your website.

Focusing Your Website

You must decide where the focus of your portfolio site will be. For example, if you aspire to be a sound designer, you should include a variety of clips and examples of the audio design you are interested in pursuing. Similarly, if you aspire to work on music, you should provide musically-oriented clips. If your goal is to work in implementation and middleware, provide files in the format of your respective middleware application, or create a screen recording of a walk-through, emphasizing the interactive aspects of your project. It is not a bad idea to demonstrate versatility if you are interested in several fields. Today's employers like an employee who can handle a variety of tasks.

Including Your Resume

Do not forget to include your resume. Your resume should indicate your work experience (including freelance work) in the game industry. Provide a brief, descriptive text on the front page to explain you, your work, and your interests and expertise. Include the dates that you worked for relevant employers. Relevant work includes any full-time or part-time position that relates directly to your work on sound design. Do not include jobs washing dishes, pumping gas, or working at the checkout counter. Although these may pad the resumes of some students or entry-level candidates, they clutter your resume with material unrelated to the skills you should focus on. Again think about what your passion is and home in on that.

The Look of Your Site

The look and feel of your website involves subjective decisions that are best left to you, the designer or the web designer you might hire. There is no one way to design a website. Just make sure the site is clean, loads quickly and works!

How to Create the Website

You could write your website entirely from scratch in HTML and CSS, but it is more common to create a website with a content management system, or CMS. A CMS stores information for each page in a database and offers a GUI that allows you to manage the database entries (i.e., your individual web pages). These systems can range from extremely simplistic and graphically-oriented to incredibly complex and convoluted.

Listed below are some popular systems for creating websites. Most offer free downloads or ways to create an initial, fully functioning website. Website-building services start you with a free account to create a page with some ad support. Limitations include the amount of storage and the capacity for features such as audio- or movie-clip players, either directly or through third-party systems. You may not have the option for ads not to appear on your site.

Credit: Jeremy Engel.

WordPress

WordPress is the most common CMS and is a full-fledged website creation solution for anyone from individuals to major corporations. Although it began as blog software, later revisions have increased its usefulness for any kind of website design. It's not exactly drag-and-drop simple, but it offers a huge collection of visual themes and staggering number of third-party applications that can provide extra functioning.

Credit: Jeremy Engel.

221

Even complex, intricate sites such as CNN's website use WordPress in certain sections. One thing is for sure, though: you will need to stay on top of security issues. WordPress is not only the most popular CMS; it is also the most vulnerable to attacks, corruption, and spam links because of its popularity. It is extremely customizable and there's a huge support base as well.

Although you can host your site from Wordpress itself, it is also software that is installed by a hosting service. WordPress offers links to plans from various hosting companies who can usually host your site for a few dollars a month.

Website Builders

These sites/services offer the ability to design sites with little to no coding required. While not as powerful and extendable as a full CMS, they can be good choices for a basic website.

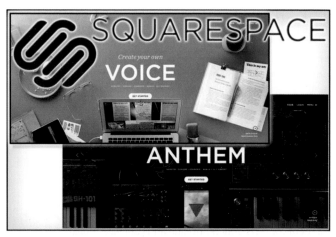

Credit: Jeremy Engel.

Go to the Classroom in the App, and click on the Video screen to get some great advice from Jim Hedges about how to break into the business!

Wix

If you have simple needs and want your website to pop and impress visually with an artistic flair, use Wix. Wix is now an HTML5 and Flash-based website builder and host with a graphic drag-and-drop interface. For a basic portfolio website, it is an excellent choice, and its editor is very easy to use for visual designers. The HTML5 Editor version does not have blog creation support, although the Flash version does. The included templates are relatively smart looking and reasonably customizable. You would likely want the Connect Domain or Combo pricing plans, both of which offer much more storage than the basic plan. They also remove the fairly visible banner ads for Wix which may be undesirable, and which come with the free version. At about $10 per month, however, the Combo plan is one of the pricier options.

Squarespace

This website and service offer very professional templates that have an extremely high quality look about them. It is also more extendible than Wix for those who might like to use it as a blog or for using it to sell products or services online. The editor is a bit clunkier to use than Wix, but also offers a lot more customization of look and feel. There is no free option but they do allow you to try the service out for 14 days for free. After that the basic website plans are $10/ month for 20 pages, and $20/month for the unlimited page individual plans. Discounts are available if you purchase a year's worth at a time.

Website Hosting Considerations

Before deciding on a particular application or service for web pages, you should compare the hosting limitations. Although many services are free initially, they often come with upload restrictions and reduced features, while paid versions offer expanded features. Although you can theoretically store all your information in separately accessible server locations and simply provide links on your web page, this practice becomes potentially difficult for some types of media in certain situations.

The Importance of Networking

If you have ever seriously researched job openings in any field, you know how vitally important networking is. To get work in an industry, you must establish a set of contacts. Your reputation and your work quality are your meal tickets, but they mean nothing unless colleagues in the industry know about them. Chances are you will get most jobs through contacts you have built up over the years. The following networking resources may be useful.

Industry Organizations

Volunteering to do work for these various organizations can definitely help you get connections and increase opportunities for you. Enlightened self-interest is OK—just give back to the community while helping yourself. This is a very natural thing to do, really. There are a ton of organizations you can join and volunteer your time to in the name of doing good works, giving back, and building your networks.

Pro Tip: Websites of Notable Composers and Sound Designers

Check out these links to websites of different composers and sound designers.

Steve Kirk

http://stevekirkpop.com/

The composer of the *Farmville* theme lets his music do the talking on a basic website with simple links to MP3 clips in a variety of styles. Note that he has both high-bandwidth links and low-bandwidth links to accommodate those with slower or older mobile connections.

Jeff Schmidt

http://jeff-schmidt.com/

Jeff Schmidt's site includes video clips of multiple games for which he designed sound, in addition to offering several video tutorials about the basics of FMOD. His no-nonsense direct approach to sound design can be helpful.

Roland Shaw

http://rolandshaw.wordpress.com/pc/

Roland Shaw's site is an excellent, in-depth blog with a great tutorial of FMOD and Wwise from a master sound designer who uses both. A bit fast-paced, Shaw's site features sounds he designed for games and a few references on how he created these sounds and approached adaptive mixing in each application.

Game Audio Network Guild (GANG)

http://audiogang.org

The organization features a range of members from newbies to grizzled veterans. GANG is a great resource for all things game audio related. Here you can find everything, from sample contracts and advice on pricing to panel talks and high-level networking events. GANG is an important part of the game audio community and has chapters around the world. The GANG awards ceremony for excellence in game audio and music (presented during the GDC) is the closest thing the game-audio world has to the Oscars (i.e., it offers recognition from peers and colleagues for excellent-quality work in design or originality in creating sound or music for games).

Interactive Audio Special Interest Group (IASIG)

http://iasig.org/

This group (pronounced "eye-ay-sig") sits under the umbrella of the MMA (MIDI Manufacturers Association). The main mission of the IASIG is to put the creators of interactive audio software and hardware directly in touch with the composers and designers in the field who use their tools. The IASIG does this through a structure of working groups and white papers. Part of our curriculum has been inspired by work done through the IASIG's Education Working Group. Membership for individuals is very reasonable at $50 per year and is a great place to give back to the community while also working side by side with high-level professionals in the field. The IASIG assembles for a town hall meeting and a separate social mixer once a year in March during GDC (the Game Developers Conference).

IGDA

The International Game Developers Association (IGDA) is the largest non-profit membership organization in the world and serves all individuals who create video games. As an international organization, the IGDA is a global network of collaborative projects and communities comprising individuals from all fields of game development—from programmers and producers to writers, artists, QA and of course, audio. The IGDA works via local Chapter meetings, Special Interest Groups (SIGs) and yearly events that are member supported and driven. They currently have over 90 Chapters and offer a great way to network and connect with all levels of people in the field. Whether you're a student or a seasoned veteran, the IGDA is a good organization to check out.

Websites

Below is a list of websites and online groups that cater to the needs of game audio professionals from a wide range of experiences and backgrounds. These can be awesome and useful resources for anyone in the business, but it's important to exhibit some common courtesy when asking for advice or posting. This means making sure to search the list to see if your question's already been answered, or if a post relates to an article, read the article before commenting thoughtlessly. In general, be courteous, and don't be annoying. This can also be a great opportunity to connect with individual luminaries in the field. Remember that you are establishing your reputation online when you post.

GigsinGames (GiGs)

http://gigsingames.com

A website geared toward those who want to try their hand at audio for games, GiGs lists full-time and contract jobs available in the industry.

Gamasutra

http://gamasutra.com

Gamasutra is a well-established site for everything about games, gaming, and game development. Its forums are good places to look for opportunities to create audio or music design for games and to exchange information and advice with those who do. Subscribe to the mailing list *Inside Gamasutra* to gain access to the newest tips on game creation, job hunting, open positions in the field, and more.

Game Audio/Game Audio Professionals Groups on LinkedIn

LinkedIn is becoming the go-to social website for those interested in cultivating networks of colleagues and other professionals in their fields. These two groups are dedicated to the topics of most interest to a wide range of game audio professionals, from students just getting their start, to seasoned pros looking for tips on sample libraries. Game Audio Professionals is a more regulated group, and you will require approval before becoming a member.

Game Audio Denizens Group on Facebook

And don't forget Facebook! This group is well-established and has a lot of pro game audio folks on it. They generally won't respond to portfolio links but are friendly with technical setup advice, as well as general information on best practices. This group is also a managed group, requiring approval to join.

Game Industry and Audio Related Trade Shows

We can't stress enough the importance of going to industry showcases, because you can actually get a chance at some face time with almost anyone in the industry! Here is a short list of some of the most important ones out there. There are new shows cropping up all the time, so do your research and find out what's hot!

You should plan to attend at least one per year, and yes, they do cost money. You may be able to save on the cost of the event by volunteering your time to help during the event. If you are more experienced, you can suggest papers and talks, or make yourself available to speak on panels. Don't be afraid to reach out to the organizers and let them know you are available and interested in taking part—you might just save yourself quite a bit of money and get your networking in, all at the same time.

GDC

The Game Developers Conference takes place once a year in San Francisco and is the largest and most complete game event going. In fact, it's the world's largest and longest-running professionals-only game industry event. It has branched out internationally in recent years to include trade shows in Europe and China. GDC features a multitude of lectures, panels, tutorials and round-table discussions on a comprehensive selection of game development topics. It also includes a prominent audio track where you will find a real cross section of audio developers all in one place.

AES

The Audio Engineering Society is the only professional society devoted exclusively to audio technology. Founded in the United States in 1948, the AES has grown to become an international organization that unites audio engineers, creative artists, scientists and students worldwide by promoting advances in audio and disseminating new knowledge and research. Every year, the AES runs a trade show rotating from east coast to west. Over the years the Audio Engineering Society has become ever more friendly to game audio and now runs its own track in the state of the art for game sound. The AES has over 14,000 members and supports a number of education initiatives. It is yet another great place to meet and network with professional audio folks who are movers and shakers in the field.

So, you think you're ready to schmooze with the best of them? If so, then prepare to test your knowledge **of trade shows and networking events** by going over to the App Classroom, and clicking on the Word Search book!

Networking/Skill-Polishing with Game Jams

One last thing to mention is a phenomenon known as a game jam, occasionally known as a hackathon. As competition increases in the game marketplace, game jams are a great way to gain valuable experience and connections, plus you get to work on games! Game jams happen frequently throughout the year and developers have a certain amount of time to create a complete game. Most frequently it's 48 hours, but this can vary. Game jams can happen onsite at a physical location, or virtually, online. In either case they are prime opportunities for networking with developers, game designers, animators and for practicing your craft under a tight deadline—all very important parts of your career.

A composer hard at work during the 2012 Global Game Jam in Guimarães, Portugal.
Credit: Laboratório Criação Digital (labcd) on Flickr.

Here are a couple of the game jams that occur regularly every year:

- **Global Game Jam** (late January): This is the granddaddy of them all. There is huge worldwide participation in this one. In 2012, the local participation at the San Francisco venue was over 250!
- **Ludum Dare** (three times per year): Probably the most well known of the online-based competitions/game jams, Ludum Dare has offered two options for participating since 2010. The first is a stricter competition, but the other is a more open and team-friendly jam.

A few pointers about participating in a game jam:

- **Be there on the initial day of the jam.** The first day of a game jam is by far the most important—this is when they socialize, form teams, and devise the ideas for games.
- **You don't have to be onsite the whole time (onsite jams only).** This might sound contradictory since we just discussed how important it is to be there on the first day. However, after that, it may be better for you to work from home. An onsite game jam can be a chaotic affair. Thus, you have the option of working from home and supplying your assets remotely via Dropbox, email, or some other service.
- **Be prepared for any outcome**. For a number of reasons your team may not end up finishing the game. This takes a while to get used to. After all, you're there to make music for a game and get your sounds out there in front of everyone else. However, if you think of the experience as simply getting to know a bunch of games and game developers, and networking with them, you'll more than likely have a great time, regardless of how your team's game turns out.

Conclusion

Sound for games is an exciting, growing and constantly changing field. Due to this growing demand, competition is also growing. By applying a few of the fundamental tools we have discussed in this level, and with hard work and luck, you can stay ahead of the competition. Remember, the game business evolves rapidly in lock step with the development of new and innovative technologies. Games and gamification are a fact of life in modern society, and solid audio designers are the ones who will develop the next "wow" generation of audio magic. This state of constant change and flux can feel daunting and overwhelming at times. Stay positive—the truth is, uncertainty is also a great agent of opportunity.

New platforms and software require designers who are not afraid to get out ahead of the curve and get their hands dirty. That's where you come in—simply being the first to use and understand a new tool can lead to good work and solid contracts. And always keep in mind, this is the entertainment industry! It is definitely a rollercoaster ride, propelled by word of mouth, where good news about your success travels fast, and bad news even faster. Be professional and understand the markets. And lastly, and most importantly, have fun out there!

The Interactive Quiz for this Level is available in the App. In the Classroom, click on the Quiz book to test your knowledge!

Index

Page numbers in **bold** refer to figures.